Finding the evidence: a gateway to the literature in child and adolescent mental health

Edited by Carol Joughin and Mike Shaw

The Focus Project
Research Unit, Royal College of Psychiatrists

Gaskell is an imprint of the Royal College of Psychiatrists,
17 Belgrave Square, London SW1X 8PG

British Library Cataloguing-in-Publication Data

A catalogue record for this book is available from the British Library.

ISBN 1-901242-50-1

Distributed in North America by American Psychiatric Press, Inc.

Gaskell is a registered trademark of the Royal College of Psychiatrists.

The Royal College of Psychiatrists is a registered charity (no. 228636).

Printed by Henry Ling Ltd, The Dorset Press, Dorchester, Dorset.

Acknowledgements

The FOCUS Project is funded by a grant from the Gatsby Charitable Foundation and the Department of Health (Section 64 grant award). We are grateful to the following individuals for their help in the development of this resource: Ms Catherine Ayres, Ms Claudine Fox, Miss Zoë Stagg, Professor Peter Hill, Professor Philip Graham, Dr Linda Dowdney and Dr Paul Ramchandani. We would also like to thank the contributors, who provided references from their particular areas of expertise.

Contents

Section 3

Appendix i

Appendix ii

Appendix iii

Contributors

Dr A. Bailey (autism)
Senior Lecturer, MRC Child Psychiatry Unit, Institute of Psychiatry, 16 De Crespigny Park, Denmark Hill, London SE5 8AF

Dr C. Bass (somatoform disorders)
Consultant in Liaison Psychiatry, Department of Psychological Medicine, John Radcliffe Hospital, Headley Way, Headington, Oxford OX3 9DU

Dr D. Bolton (obsessive–compulsive disorder)
Department of Psychology, Institute of Psychiatry, De Crespigny Park, Denmark Hill, London SE5 8AZ

Dr D. Di Ceglie (gender identity disorders)
Director, Adolescent Department, Tavistock Clinic, 120 Belsize Lane, London NW3 5BA

Dr E. Fombonne (self-harm and autism)
Reader in Epidemiological Child Psychiatry, MRC Child Psychiatry Unit, Institute of Psychiatry, 16 De Crespigny Park, Denmark Hill, London SE5 8AF

Professor E. Garralda (chronic fatigue syndrome)
Professor in Child and Adolescent Psychiatry, Imperial College School of Medicine, St Mary's Campus, Norfolk Place, London W2 1PG

Dr A. Gillcrest (Asperger's syndrome)
Senior Lecturer in Child and Adolescent Psychiatry, Young People's Department, Royal Cornhill Hospital, Cornhill Road, Aberdeen AB25 2ZH

Dr D. Glaser (emotional and physical/sexual abuse)
Consultant Psychiatrist, Department of Psychological Medicine, Great Ormond Street Children's Hospital, Great Ormond Street, London WC1N 3JH

Dr J. Green (Asperger's syndrome)
Consultant Psychiatrist, Dept of Child and Family Psychiatry, Booth Hall Children's Hospital, Charlestown Road, Blackley, Manchester M9 7AA

Professor R. Harrington (depression)
Professor of Child and Adolescent Psychiatry, Royal Manchester Children's Hospital, Hospital Road, Pendlebury, Manchester M27 4HA

Mr M. Heiman (group therapy)
Senior Clinical Nurse Specialist, Child and Adolescent Mental Health Services, Clare House, Blackshaw Road, London SW17 0QT

Professor P. Hill (attention–deficit hyperactivity disorder)
Department of Psychological Medicine, Great Ormond Street Children's Hospital, Great Ormond Street, London WC1N 3JH

Dr C. Hollis (schizophrenia)
Senior Lecturer in Child and Adolescent Psychiatrist, Department of Child and Adolescent Psychiatry, Queens Medical Centre, Clifton Boulevard, Nottingham NG7 2UH

Dr C. Kelly (elimination)
Consultant Child Psychiatrist, Central Health Clinic, East Park Terrace, Southampton SO14 0YL

Dr B. Lask (eating disorders)
Reader, Eating Disorders Research Team, St George's Hospital Medical School, Department of Psychiatry, Cranmer Terrace, Tooting, London SW17 0RE

Ms C. Maynerd (family therapy)
Head of Family Therapy, Cotswold House, Sutton Hospital, Cotswold Road, Surrey SM2 5NF

Dr M. Newman (post-traumatic stress disorder)
Consultant Child Psychiatrist, William Harvey Clinic, 313–315 Cortis Road, Putney, London SW15 6XG

Dr S. Pettle (dying child)
Consultant Clinical Psychologist, Child and Family Consultation Centre, 1 Wolverton Gardens, London W6 7DQ

Dr P. Reader (parenting assessment)
Consultant Child Psychiatrist, Child and Family Consultation Centre, 1 Wolverton Gardens, London W6 7DQ

Ms J. Robarts (music therapy)
Nordoff Robbins Music Therapy Centre, 2 Lissenden Gardens, London NW5 1PP

Professor M. Robertson (Gilles de la Tourette syndrome)
University College London Medical School, Department of Psychiatry and Behavioural Sciences, Wolfson Building, Riding House Street, London W1N 8AA

Dr S. Scott (conduct disorder)
Senior Lecturer and Consultant in Child Psychiatry, Institute of Psychiatry, 16 De Crespigny Park, Denmark Hill, London SE5 8AF

Dr D. Steinberg (consultation)
Consultant Psychiatrist, Adolescent Service and Young People's Unit, Ticehurst House Hospital, Ticehurst, Nr Wadhurst, Sussex TN5 7HU

Dr J. Trowell (sexual abuse)
Consultant Psychiatrist, Child and Family Department, Tavistock Clinic, 120 Belsize Lane, London NW3 5BA

Dr J. Turk (dementia)
Consultant Child Psychiatrist, St George's Hospital Medical School, Jenner Wing, Cranmer Terrace, London SW17 0RE

Dr G. Wannan (mania)
Specialist Registrar, Merton Child, Adolescent and Family Service, Cricket Green Polyclinic, 4 Birches Close, Cricket Green, Mitcham, Surrey CR4 4LQ

Professor S. Wessely (chronic fatigue syndrome)
Professor of Epidemiological and Liaison Psychiatry, Institute of Psychiatry, Denmark Hill, London SE5 8AZ

Mr R. White (legislation)
White and Sherwin Solicitors, Simpson House, 2–6 Cherry Orchard Road, Croydon, Surrey CR0 6BA

Dr A. York (depression)
Consultant Child Psychiatrist, Child and Family Consultation Centre, Richmond Royal Hospital, Kew Foot Road, London TW7 2TE

Introduction: the editors' goals and plans

There is an unprecedented demand for scientific evidence in child and adolescent mental health. Clinicians are under pressure to keep up-to-date and demonstrate that their decisions are based on the best available evidence. Families are hungry for information about their children's difficulties and what they can do to help or get help. Similarly, policy-makers and health service commissioners need a rational basis for prioritising service developments.

Electronic tools, such as the internet, offer immediate access to a huge and rapidly expanding child and adolescent mental health literature. Without a critical guide there is a danger of being overwhelmed by the sheer volume of information.

Finding the Evidence is a new type of publication, with three main aims. First, to identify the best available scientific evidence, second, to promote critical appraisal, and finally, to be scrupulously up-to-date.

In this first edition of *Finding the Evidence* we have used two methods to select the evidence.First, electronic search strategies were applied to identify all relevant systematic reviews, meta-analyses and clinical guidelines. Second, experts were asked to choose (non-systematic) reviews and cutting edge and classic papers and books.

As the term implies, systematic reviews weigh the evidence using systematic criteria to minimise error and bias. Meta-analyses merge and re-analyse the results of studies that are sufficiently similar and robust. Clinical guidelines should be systematically developed for use in specific clinical situations.

High quality systematic reviews, meta-analyses and clinical guidelines are, scientifically, extremely valuable. Unfortunately, this type of systematic evidence is very limited in the child and adolescent mental health literature. For this reason we have included all the systematic reviews, meta-analyses and clinical guidelines found (see comments below about critical appraisal and future editions).

Readers are invited to let us know about any systematic reviews, meta-analyses and clinical guidelines we have overlooked. (There is a tear-off form at the back of the book, or contact us at FOCUS at the address shown on the form.)

To explore the literature further we have taken advice from researchers, academics and practitioners with a special interest in each field. This has been the basis on which we have selected reviews, where the evidence has been weighed on the basis of the author's personal opinion, rather than explicit systematic criteria. Cutting edge papers present important new theories and evidence, while classic papers are landmark publications of enduring interest.

Not all topics fit neatly into this framework and we have been flexible where appropriate. For example, we have used very different headings for the section on consent to treatment. Scientific evidence is developing much more quickly and is far more advanced in some areas. Thus, while a paper on suicide published in 1996 is considered a classic, the scientific literature on music therapy is at a much earlier stage of development. We have been extremely fortunate in receiving advice from internationally renowned experts and in some areas advice from more than one expert. We are keen to extend the range of expert advice in the future.

No list can be exhaustive and *Finding the Evidence* points readers in the right direction. Section 1 provides guidance on electronic search strategies, while Section 2 presents the evidence and has suggestions on where to find more about specific topics. Section 3 provides evidence on important emerging datasets.

All evidence needs to be critically examined, and Appendix ii provides a range of critical appraisal tools. Future editions will include our own critical appraisals of the papers cited. We are likely to start with the systematic reviews, meta-analyses and cutting edge papers.

We are committed to keeping *Finding the Evidence* up-to-date, by continually renewing the searches, adding to the expert advice and acting on the suggestions of readers. An important step in this direction will be to publish *Finding the Evidence* on the internet. This will allow new material to be available without delay, and be an ideal medium for publishing the critical appraisals.

Ultimately, it should be possible for internet users to browse the recommended papers, picking out the critical appraisals they are particularly interested in. The full text could then be accessed using internet links to the article's publishers.

We are very aware there are gaps in the subject areas covered. We see the first edition of *Finding the Evidence* as a starting point on which to build. Future editions will strengthen the review of diagnostic categories and therapeutic approaches and include areas such as child development and developmental psychopathology. We are looking to add new topics to each edition and would value readers' views on what to include.

Initially, *Finding the Evidence* will be of most value to clinicians, trainees and policy-makers. However, it is possible for *Finding the Evidence* to be relevant to all disciplines contributing to child and adolescent mental health care, as well as carers and/or relatives.

We envisage *Finding the Evidence* as a 'living document' evolving to address the growing demand for knowledge and exploit the new opportunities provided by information technology.

Mike Shaw and Carol Joughin

Section 1: a guide to finding the evidence

A description of terms

Systematic reviews

The term 'systematic review' implies that a review has been prepared using a systematic approach to minimise bias and random errors. Systematic reviews differ from other reviews in that they adhere to a documented, transparent structure. Rather than reflecting the views of the author or a selection of published literature they should be comprehensive (University of York NHS Centre for Reviews and Dissemination, 1996). They aim to establish whether scientific findings are consistent and can be generalised across populations and whether the findings differ significantly by particular subsets. Meta-analyses are undertaken in some systematic reviews if the data is considered to be robust and the studies are sufficiently similar in design to allow for the findings to be merged and re-analysed as a single cohort. However, the reader should be aware that not all researchers will have taken a systematic approach to the development of their meta-analysis and this can lead to significant bias. We have provided tools in Appendix ii, which will help you to appraise the quality of the research.

For the purposes of this list we have searched Medline, PsychLit and the Cochrane Library for systematic reviews and meta-analyses using defined search strategies (see Appendix i). The systematic reviews, which have been found on the Cochrane database, have been marked so that readers can access the Cochrane review of the systematic review.

More about Cochrane

The Cochrane Collaboration is an international organisation that aims to help people make well-informed decisions about health care by preparing, maintaining and promoting the accessibility of systematic reviews of the effects of health care interventions. The Cochrane Collaboration produces the Cochrane Library, which is a collection of databases, published on-line as well as on CD-ROM, and updated on a quarterly basis. The Cochrane Library consists of the Cochrane Database of Systematic Reviews (CDSR), the Database of Abstracts of Reviews of Effectiveness (DARE), the Cochrane Controlled Trials Register (CCTR) and the Cochrane Review Methodology Database.

○ The Cochrane Database of Systematic Reviews is the main product of the Cochrane Collaboration. It brings together all the currently available Cochrane Reviews and also gives details of protocols for systematic reviews, which have been registered with the Cochrane Collaboration. We have included protocols for systematic reviews in Section 2.

○ The Database of Abstracts of Reviews of Effectiveness (DARE) is a collection of abstracts of quality assessed systematic reviews, other assessed reviews and bibliographic references. DARE is produced by the NHS Centre for Reviews and Dissemination at the University of York.

○ The Cochrane Controlled Trials Register (CCTR) includes references to clinical trials compiled by the Cochrane Review Groups. These trials have been judged as meeting certain quality standards.

Collaborative Review Groups

Cochrane Collaborative Review Groups consist of individuals who share an interest in a particular area of health care. Their main purpose is to prepare and maintain systematic reviews of relevance to the group. The main collaborative review group of relevance to child and adolescent mental health is the Developmental, Psychosocial and Learning Problems Group. They plan to address a range of medical, social, educational and socio-legal problems, which will cover developmental and psychosocial problems of childhood and adolescence, including juvenile delinquency; learning problems (including, but not restricted to learning disabilities); and personality disorders and adult offending.

Where possible, sections in this resource give the contact name and details for the relevant Cochrane Collaborative Review Group.

Clinical practice guidelines

These consist of a series of systematically developed statements to assist patients and practitioners when making decisions about appropriate health care in specified clinical circumstances. They should be based on information from systematic reviews and incorporate the views of clinicians and patients. However, not all clinical guidelines have been developed using a robust approach and readers should therefore use the critical appraisal tool in Appendix ii before using the information to inform their practice.

A database of critically appraised guidelines has been established in Oxford and Anglia and is available at **http://www.his.ox.ac.uk/guidelines/index.html**

A guide to searching

The list in Section 2 provides a starting point for finding relevant research information. If you wish to search for more information we would suggest the following approach. Please remember that this is a very basic guide and is not a substitute for a training session with your local librarian!

○ **Step 1. Medline and Psychlit search.**
These are still the best databases to start with. However, for general therapy questions, the Cochrane Library now contains more controlled trials than Medline. For systematic reviews and meta-analyses use the search strategy given in Appendix i. If you are doing a more extensive search remember to look in Embase. This will give you a wider choice of European journals.

○ **Step 2. Cochrane Library.**
This is available on CD-ROM and will give you access to systematic reviews, protocols for systematic reviews in development, information from DARE and primary studies from the CCTR.

○ **Step 3. Clinical practice guidelines.**
For clinical practice guidelines try the National Guideline Clearing House: **http://www.guidelines.gov**. Also for guidelines check the Scottish

Intercollegiate Guidelines Network: **http://www.show.scot.nhs.UK/sign/home.htm** or critically appraised guidelines at: **http://www.his.ox.ac.uk/guidelines/index.html**

More about Medline

Medline is compiled by the National Library of Medicine of the US and indexes over 4000 journals published in over 70 countries. It lists about 300 000 articles per year and covers all areas of medicine, including nursing, psychiatry, psychology, biochemistry and health care management. It does not include books or conference abstracts (even if they are printed in journals indexed on Medline).

Medline is available in three forms:

○ A printed version – *Index Medicus*

○ On-line – from 1996 to date. This can be accessed on the internet by a number of servers.

○ CD-ROM – this may be accessed in libraries on between 10 and 18 CDs. Many trusts have also made it available through the local networks to offices and clinical areas.

A number of different companies sell Medline and so slightly different commands are required depending on the supplier. Two of the most common suppliers are Ovid Technologies (OVID) and SilverPlatter Information Ltd (WinSPIRS).

Medline and Psychlit will supply you with the authors, title, research institution and an abstract of the paper.

Ways of searching

You can search for articles in two ways. By **textword**. This will give you any word, which is listed on the database. It will include the title, abstract, authors' names or institute where the research was performed. By **MeSH heading**. Medline and Psychlit use a thesaurus to make searching more effective. A thesaurus is a controlled vocabulary, which is used to index information from journals. It groups related concepts using a single preferred term. Medline and the Cochrane Library both use a thesaurus called MeSH. MeSH contains approximately 17 000 terms. Each term represents a single concept appearing in the literature. Using OVID, MeSH headings can be identified by using a 'mapping' procedure. When using SilverPlatter they can be identified by checking the thesaurus or using the 'suggest' option. Sometimes you will not be able to find a MeSH term to match your subject. If this is the case you will need to search using textwords. However do remember that when searching on textwords the database will be searched for exactly the term that you have entered. You will, therefore, need to remember to consider all possible spellings and terms to describe your subject.

Exploding!

The MeSH terms are arranged in hierarchical structures called trees. They start with a broad term and divide into branches of more specific terms (see Table 1, page 6).

Database indexers are instructed to use the most specific term(s) available when indexing papers. During the mapping process you will first be offered the most general term and then the more specific term (if available). The tree structure allows you to explode your search. Exploding helps you obtain comprehensive coverage of your subject area. You can search for your MeSH term plus all its narrower terms at the same time.

Table 1. Example of a MeSH Tree

O   Eating disorders

     O   Anorexia nervosa

     O   Hyperphagia

        O   Bulimia

     O   Pica

Major headings

As many as 20 MeSH terms are assigned by indexers to any one article. Some headings are designated as major headings; these represent the main concepts of a paper. These major headings are prefaced by an asterisk * and help distinguish articles which discuss your subject in detail from those which discuss it briefly.

Boolean operators

Boolean operators can be used to combine together keywords in your search strategy. AND allows you to link together different subjects; it focuses your search and you will retrieve fewer papers. For example, by searching for sexual abuse AND conduct disorder you will only identify papers which address both issues together. OR allows you to broaden your search. If you search for sexual abuse OR conduct disorder you will identify papers which address either sexual abuse or conduct disorder or both issues.

NOT should be used with care, but could be used to identify papers which for example address hyperkinetic disorder but not conduct disorder (hyperkinetic disorder NOT conduct disorder).

Further refining your search

The abstract may be searched for areas of interest in the text: for example, keying in random* will pick up randomise, randomised and randomisation if you are looking for a randomised controlled trial (RCT).

Searching for terms in a particular field (e.g. author or title)

If you are trying to track down a paper and you know a few details you can search by using field suffixes such as:

.ab   Word in abstract

.au   Author

.pt   Publication type

.sh   Subject heading (MeSH)

.tw   Word in title or abstract

These are OVID suffixes but the ones in SilverPlatter are very similar.

If you are looking for a paper on child sexual abuse and you know it was published in the *Journal of the American Academy of Child and Adolescent Psychiatry* simply enter:

○ Child sexual abuse.ti
  .ti shows that the term is in the title

○ Journal of the American Academy of Child and Adolescent Psychiatry.jn
  .jn shows that this is the journal you are looking for

○ Then combine the two instructions #1 AND #2

Sensitivity and specificity

Sensitivity is the likelihood of retrieving 'relevant' items; specificity is the likelihood of excluding 'irrelevant' items. To increase the sensitivity and so increase the records retrieved:

○ Broaden your question

○ Try to use more search terms (look at the papers that you already have and see what they have used)

○ Use truncation (* or $) in textword searches

○ Add in and combine terms of related meaning using OR

○ Use the word NEAR to retrieve terms in the same sentence

○ Use the 'explode' feature

○ Select 'all subheadings' with MeSH terms

○ Extend the dates of publication.

To increase the specificity of your search and so reduce the number of papers retrieved:

○ Narrow your question

○ Use more specific terms in a textword search

○ Use MeSH terms rather than a textword search

○ Use more specific MeSH terms

○ Add in terms using AND to represent other areas of your question

○ Limit to a particular language or publication type, e.g., randomised controlled trial or meta-analysis.

Quick tip

The search strategy in Appendix i will allow you to pick up the maximum possible number of randomised controlled trials. This can be saved on disc and used again and again for different searches. We have also provided a search strategy for systematic reviews and meta-analyses.

Search terms and truncation

At the end of each section we have added suggested search terms and the number of primary research papers that you will be able to access if you search on the CCTR. Always remember to try alternative spellings for words such as 'behaviour'; using 'behavior' will usually generate many more hits. Other useful tips include using parentheses to link words together and using an asterisk to ensure that all words with the same beginning are included. For example 'child*' will include child, child's and children.

References and suggested further reading

Greenhalgh T. (1997) *How to Read a Paper: The Basics of Evidence-Based Medicine*. London: BMJ Publishing Group.

University of York NHS Centre for Reviews and Dissemination (1996) *Undertaking Systematic Reviews of Research on Effectiveness*. CRD Report No 4. York: NHS Centre for Reviews and Dissemination.

Finding the evidence: summary

1. Compose a clinical question. This should focus your search and ensure it is appropriate.

Remember to define: (a) the population or type of patient (age, gender, diagnosis etc.); (b) the intervention or exposure; and (c) the outcome of interest.

Example

In girls between the ages of 3 and 9 with conduct disorder, do parent training programmes improve the child's attendance at school?

2. Identify relevant databases to search

Consider Medline, Psychlit, Cochrane Library and also sites such as the HTA site for key reports and the National Guidelines Clearing House for clinical guidelines (see Step 3 in previous section).

3. Identify search terms for each component of the question. Always remember possible alternative spellings and terms.

Remember to use textwords and MeSH headings.

Example

When searching for conduct disorder, also consider using: behavioural problem*, antisocial behaviour, antisocial behavior and behaviour disorder*.

4. Determine your Boolean operators, such as AND, OR or NOT.

These allow you to define the papers that you are interested in.

Example

If you are looking for papers which discussed girls and not boys with hyper-kinetic disorder you could put: child* AND girl* NOT boy* AND hyperkinetic disorder.

5. Adjust your search strategy to further limit the search if you have too many citations or broaden it if you have too few.

Consider limiting to English language or a more specific term for the condition. See section on sensitivity and specificity.

Section 2: the evidence

Directory

This section is organised by diagnostic categories and therapeutic approaches. The evidence is presented through systematic reviews, meta-analyses, clinical guidelines, reviews, reports and cutting edge and classic papers. Suggestions on where to find out more about specific topics are also included.

This directory lists diagnostic categories and therapeutic approaches by frequently used terms, in alphabetical order. These terms will direct the reader to the appropriate section.

ADD	see ATTENTION-DEFICIT HYPERACTIVITY DISORDER
ADHD	see ATTENTION-DEFICIT HYPERACTIVITY DISORDER
abnormal illness behaviour	see PAEDIATRIC LIAISON: somatoform disorder
abuse	see ABUSE: emotional and physical and ABUSE: sexual
affective disorders	see EMOTIONAL DISORDERS: depression, and PSYCHOSIS: mania, and bipolar affective disorder
aggression	see CONDUCT DISORDER: disruptive/ aggressive behaviour, and CONDUCT DISORDER: juvenile delinquency
alcohol	see SUBSTANCE MISUSE
amphetamines	see ATTENTION-DEFICIT HYPERACTIVITY DISORDER
anorexia nervosa	see EATING DISORDERS
antidepressant drugs	see EMOTIONAL DISORDERS: depression
antisocial behaviour	see CONDUCT DISORDER: disruptive/ aggressive behaviour, and CONDUCT DISORDER: juvenile delinquency
anxiety	see EMOTIONAL DISORDERS: anxiety and phobia
Asperger's syndrome	see PERVASIVE DEVELOPMENT DISORDERS
assessment	see EMERGING DATASETS: assessment
attachment disorders	see EMERGING DATASETS: attachment disorders

attention-deficit hyperactivity disorder	see ATTENTION-DEFICIT HYPERACTIVITY DISORDER
autism	see PERVASIVE DEVELOPMENTAL DISORDERS: autism, and PAEDIATRIC LIAISON: dementia
behaviour problems	see CONDUCT DISORDER: disruptive/ aggressive behaviour, and CONDUCT DISORDER: juvenile delinquency
bipolar affective disorder	see PSYCHOSIS: mania and bipolar affective disorder
body image	see EATING DISORDERS
brain disorders	see PAEDIATRIC LIAISON: dementia
bulimia nervosa	see EATING DISORDERS
CAMHS	see ORGANISATION OF CAMHS
challenging behaviour	see CONDUCT DISORDER: disruptive/ aggressive behaviour, and CONDUCT DISORDER: juvenile delinquency
child mental health services	see ORGANISATION OF CAMHS
child protection	see LEGAL ISSUES: legislation, and LEGAL ISSUES: parenting assessment
Children Act 1988	see LEGAL ISSUES: legislation, and LEGAL ISSUES: consent and competence
chronic fatigue syndrome	see PAEDIATRIC LIAISON: chronic fatigue syndrome
competence	see LEGAL ISSUES: consent and competence
compulsions	see EMOTIONAL DISORDERS: obsessive– compulsive disorder
conduct disorder	see CONDUCT DISORDER: disruptive aggressive behaviour
consent to treatment	see LEGAL ISSUES: consent and competence
constipation	see ELIMINATION
consultation	see CONSULTATION
conversion disorder	see PAEDIATRIC LIAISON: somatoform disorder
court reports	see LEGAL ISSUES: legislation, and LEGAL ISSUES: parenting assessment
crime	see CONDUCT DISORDER: juvenile delinquency
DSH	see DELIBERATE SELF-HARM
death	see PAEDIATRIC LIAISON: dying child
deliberate self-harm	see DELIBERATE SELF-HARM
delinquency	see CONDUCT DISORDER: juvenile delinquency

dementia	see PAEDIATRIC LIAISON: dementia
depression	see EMOTIONAL DISORDERS: depression
depressive feelings	see EMOTIONAL DISORDERS: depression
diagnosis	see EMERGING DATASETS: assessment
dieting	see EATING DISORDERS
disintegrative psychosis	see PAEDIATRIC LIAISON: dementia
disruptive behaviour	see CONDUCT DISORDERS: disruptive/ aggressive behaviour, and CONDUCT DISORDERS: juvenile delinquency
drug abuse	see SUBSTANCE MISUSE
dying child	see PAEDIATRIC LIAISON: dying child
ECT	see EMERGING DATASETS: electroconvulsive therapy
eating disorders	see EATING DISORDERS
electroconvulsive therapy	see EMERGING DATASETS: electroconvulsive therapy
emotional abuse	see ABUSE: emotional and physical
emotional disorders	see EMOTIONAL DISORDERS
encephalitis	see PAEDIATRIC LIAISON: dementia
encopresis	see ELIMINATION
enuresis	see ELIMINATION
family therapy	see THERAPEUTIC APPROACHES: family therapy
fatigue	see PAEDIATRIC LIAISON: chronic fatigue syndrome
fear	see EMOTIONAL DISORDERS: anxiety and phobia
gender identity disorders	see GENDER IDENTITY DISORDERS
Gilles de la Tourette syndrome	see TIC DISORDERS
glue-sniffing	see SUBSTANCE MISUSE
group therapy	see THERAPEUTIC APPROACHES: group therapy
health services	see ORGANISATION OF CAMHS
heroin	see SUBSTANCE MISUSE
hyperactivity	see ATTENTION-DEFICIT HYPERACTIVITY DISORDER
hyperkinetic disorder	see ATTENTION-DEFICIT HYPERACTIVITY DISORDER
hypochondriasis	see PAEDIATRIC LIAISON: somatoform disorder
hypomania	see PSYCHOSIS: mania and bipolar affective disorder

infantile psychosis	see PERVASIVE DEVELOPMENT DISORDERS: autism
legislation	see LEGAL ISSUES: legislation, and LEGAL ISSUES: consent and competence
ME	see PAEDIATRIC LIAISON: chronic fatigue syndrome
mania	see PSYCHOSIS: mania and bipolar affective disorder
mental health services	see ORGANISATION OF CAMHS
mood disorders	see EMOTIONAL DISORDERS: anxiety and phobia, and EMOTIONAL DISORDERS: depression
music therapy	see THERAPEUTIC APPROACHES: music therapy
myalgic encephalomyelitis	see PAEDIATRIC LIAISON: chronic fatigue syndrome
neglect	see ABUSE: emotional and physical
non-accidental injury	see ABUSE: emotional and physical
OCD	see EMOTIONAL DISORDERS: obsessive–compulsive disorder
ODD	see CONDUCT DISORDERS: disruptive/ aggressive behaviour
obesity	see EATING DISORDERS
obsessional disorders	see EMOTIONAL DISORDERS: obsessive–compulsive disorder
oppositional defiant disorder	see CONDUCT DISORDERS: disruptive/ aggressive behaviour
organisation of health services	see ORGANISATION OF CAMHS
overweight	see EATING DISORDERS
PTSD	see POST-TRAUMATIC STRESS DISORDER
panic	see EMOTIONAL DISORDERS
parasuicide	see DELIBERATE SELF-HARM
parental	see LEGAL ISSUES: parenting assessment
pervasive developmental disorder	see PERVASIVE DEVELOPMENT DISORDERS: autism, and PERVASIVE DEVELOPMENT DISORDERS: Asperger's syndrome
phobias	see EMOTIONAL DISORDERS
physical abuse	see ABUSE: emotional and physical
post-traumatic stress disorder	see POST-TRAUMATIC STRESS DISORDER
prevention	see EMERGING DATASETS: prevention and mental health promotion

ABUSE: emotional and physical

Systematic reviews and meta-analyses

Stevenson J (1999) **The treatment of the long-term sequelae of child abuse**. *Journal of Child Psychology and Psychiatry and Allied Disciplines*, **40**, 89–111.

Clinical guidelines

American Academy of Child and Adolescent Psychiatry (1997) **Practice parameters for the forensic evaluation of children and adolescents who may have been physically or sexually abused**. *Journal of American Academy of Child and Adolescent Psychiatry*, **36** (suppl.), 37S–56S.

Stevenson J (1999) **The treatment of the long-term sequalae of child abuse**. *Journal of Child Psychology and Psychiatry*, **40**, 89–111.

Reviews

Cicchetti D & Nurcombe B (eds) (1991) **Special edition devoted to defining psychological maltreatment**. *Development and Psychopathology*, **3**, 1–124.

Cohn A D & Davro D (1987) **Is treatment too late: what 10 years of evaluative research tells us**. *Child Abuse and Neglect*, **11**, 433–442.

Glaser D & Prior V (1997) **Is the term 'child protection' applicable to emotional abuse?** *Child Abuse Review*, **6**, 315–329.

Hart S, Binggeli N & Brassard M (1998) **Evidence for the effects for psychological maltreatment**. *Journal of Emotional Abuse*, **1**, 27–58.

Macmillan H L, MacMillan J H, Offord D R, *et al* (1994) **Primary prevention of child physical abuse and neglect: a critical review: Part I**. *Journal of Child Psychology and Psychiatry*, **34**, 835–836.

Classic papers

Skuse D H (1984) **Extreme deprivation in early childhood: diverse outcomes for three siblings from an extraordinary family**. *Journal of Child Psychology and Psychiatry*, **25**, 523–541.

—— (1984) **Extreme deprivation in early childhood: theoretical issues and a comparative review**. *Journal of Child Psychology and Psychiatry*, **25**, 543–572.

Cutting edge papers

Claussen A H & Crittenden P M (1991) **Physical and psychological maltreatment: relations among types of maltreatment**. *Child Abuse and Neglect*, **15**, 5–18.

Gibbons J, Gallagher B, Bell C, *et al* (1995) ***Development After Physical Abuse in Early Childhood: a Follow–Up Study of Children on Protection Registers***. London: HMSO.

Books

Briere J, Berliner L, Bulkley J A, *et al* (1996) *The ASPAC Handbook on Child Maltreatment*. Thousand Oaks, CA: Sage Publications.

Garabino J, Guttmann E & Seeley J (1986) *The Psychologically Battered Child*. San Francisco, CA: Jossey–Bass.

Glaser D (1995) **Emotionally abusive experiences**. In *Assessment of Parenting: Psychiatric and Psychological Contributions* (eds P Reder & C Lucey), pp. 73–86. London: Routledge.

Cochrane Controlled Trials Register
0 hits (keywords: child* AND "physical abuse*")

Cochrane Developmental, Psychosocial and Learning Problems Group
Contact: Ms Jane Dennis, Bristol, UK. E-mail: J.Dennis@bristol.ac.uk

ABUSE: sexual

Systematic reviews and meta-analyses

De-Jong T I & Gorey K M (1996) **Short-term versus long-term group work with female survivors of childhood sexual abuse: a brief meta-analytic review**. *Social Work with Groups*, **19**, 19–27.

Finkelhor D & Berliner L (1995) **Research on the treatment of sexually abused children: a review and recommendations**. *Journal of the American Academy of Child and Adolescent Psychiatry*, **34**, 1408–1423. Reviewed on DARE.

Jones D & Ramchandani P (1999) *Child Sexual Abuse*. Oxford: Radcliffe Medical Press.

Jumper S A (1995) **A meta-analysis of the relationship of child sexual abuse to adult psychological adjustment**. *Child Abuse and Neglect*, **19**, 715–728.

Neumann D A, Houskamp B M, Pollock V E, *et al* (1996) **The long-term sequelae of childhood sexual abuse in women: a meta-analytic review**. *Child Maltreatment: Journal of the American Professional Society on the Abuse of Children*, **1**, 6–16.

Reeker J, Ensing D & Elliott R (1997) **A meta-analytic investigation of group treatment outcomes for sexually abused children**. *Child Abuse and Neglect*, **21**, 669–680. Reviewed on DARE.

Rind B & Tromovitch P (1997) A **meta-analytic review of findings from national samples on psychological correlates of child sexual abuse**. *Journal of Sex Research*, **34**, 237–255.

——, Tromovitch P & Bauserman R (1998) **A meta-analytic examination of assumed properties of child sexual abuse using college samples**. *Psychological Bulletin*, **124**, 22–53.

Rispens J, Aleman A & Goudena P P (1997) **Prevention of child sexual abuse victimisation: a meta-analysis of school programs**. *Child Abuse and Neglect*, **21**, 975–987.

West M (1998) **Meta-analysis of studies assessing the efficacy of projective techniques in discriminating child sexual abuse**. *Child Abuse and Neglect*, **22**, 1151–1166.

Wonderlich S A, Brewerton T D, Jocic J, *et al* (1997) **Relationship of childhood sexual abuse and eating disorders**. *Journal of the American Academy of Child and Adolescent Psychiatry*, **36**, 1107–1115.

Clinical guidelines

American Academy of Child and Adolescent Psychiatry (1997) **Practice parameters for the forensic evaluation of children and adolescents who may have been physically or sexually abused**. *Journal of American Academy of Child and Adolescent Psychiatry*, **36** (suppl.) 37S–56S.

Royal College of Psychiatrists (1993) *Child Psychiatry and Child Sexual Abuse*. Council Report CR24. London: Royal College of Psychiatrists.

Sharland E, Seal H, Croucher M, *et al* (1996) *Professional Intervention in Child Sexual Abuse*. London: The Stationery Office.

Reviews

Alvarez A (1989) *Child Sexual Abuse: the Need to Remember and the Need to Forget. The Consequences of Child Sexual Abuse*. Occasional papers No. 3. London: Association of Child Psychology and Psychiatry.

Beitchman J H, Zucker K J, Hood J E, *et al* (1991) **A review of short-term effects of child sexual abuse.** *Child Abuse and Neglect*, **15**, 537–556.

—, —, —, *et al* (1992) **A review of the long-term effects of child sexual abuse.** *Child Abuse and Neglect*, **16**, 101–118.

Kendall-Tackett K A, William L M & Finkelhor D (1993) **Impact of sexual abuse on children: a review and synthesis of recent empirical studies.** *Psychological Bulletin*, **113**, 164–180.

Sinason V (1988) **Smiling, swallowing, sickening and stupefying. The effect of abuse on the child.** *Psychoanalytic Psychotherapy*, **3**, 97–111.

Stevenson J (1999) **The treatment of the long-term sequalae of child abuse.** *Journal of Child Psychology and Psychiatry*, **40**, 89–111.

Trowell J (1997) **Child sexual abuse.** In *Rooted Sorrows* (ed. Hon. Justice Wall), pp. 20–33. Bristol: Family Law.

Classic papers

Finkelhor D & Browne A (1985) **The traumatic impact of child sexual abuse: a conceptualisation.** *American Journal of Orthopsychiatry*, **55**, 530–541.

Fredrick W N, Grambsch P, Broughton D, *et al* (1991) **Normal sexual behaviour in children.** *Journal of Paediatrics*, **88**, 456–464.

McLeer S V, Deblinger E, Atkins M S, *et al* (1988) **Post-traumatic stress disorder in sexually abused children.** *Journal of the American Academy of Child and Adolescent Psychiatry*, **27**, 650–654.

Summit R (1983) **The child sexual abuse accommodation syndrome.** *Child Abuse and Neglect*, **7**, 177–193.

Cutting edge papers

Lanktree C & Briere J (1995) **Outcome for therapy of sexually abused children: a repeated measure study.** *Child Abuse and Neglect*, **19**, 329–334.

Skuse D, Bentovim A, Hodges J, *et al* (1998) **Risk factors for development of sexually abusive behaviour in sexually victimised adolescent boys.** *British Medical Journal*, **317**, 175–179.

Tebbitt J, Swanston H, Oates, *et al* (1997) **Five years after child sexual abuse, persisting dysfunction and problems of prediction.** *Journal of American Academy of Child and Adolescent Psychiatry*, **36**, 330–339.

Books

Bentovim A, Elton A, Hildebrand J, *et al* (1988) *Child Sexual Abuse in the Family*. London: Wright Butterworth Press.

Furniss T (1991) *Multi–Professional Handbook of Child Sexual Abuse*. London: Routledge.

Glaser D & Frosh S (1993) *Child Sexual Abuse* (2nd edn). London: Macmillan.

Kemple R & Kemple H (1984) *The Common Secret Sexual Abuse of Child and Adolescents*. San Francisco, CA: Freeman Press.

Segroi S (1982) *Handbook of Clinical Interventions in Child Sexual Abuse*. Lexington, MA: Lexington Books.

Cochrane Controlled Trials Register
61 hits (keywords: child* AND abuse* AND sex*)

Cochrane Developmental, Psychosocial and Learning Problems Group
Contact: Ms Jane Dennis, Bristol, UK. E-mail: J.Dennis@bristol.ac.uk

Systematic reviews and meta-analyses

Faraone S, Faraone V & Biederman J (1994) **Is attention-deficit hyperactivity disorder familial?** *Harvard Review of Psychiatry*, **1**, 271–287.

Gaub M & Carlson C L (1997) **Gender differences in ADHD: a meta-analysis and critical review**. *Journal of the American Academy of Child and Adolescent Psychiatry*, **36**, 1036–1045. (Erratum in **36**, 1783.)

Kavale K (1982) **The efficacy of stimulant drug treatment for hyperactivity: a meta-analysis**. *Journal of Learning Disabilities*, **15**, 280–289.

—— & Forness S R (1983) **Hyperactivity and diet treatment: a meta-analysis of the Feingold hypothesis**. *Journal of Learning Disabilities*, **16**, 324–330.

Losier B J, McGrath P J & Klein R M (1996) **Error patterns on the continuous performance test in non-medicated and medicated samples of children with and without ADHD: a meta-analytic review**. *Journal of Child Psychology and Psychiatry*, **37**, 971–987. Reviewed on DARE.

Miller A, Lee S, Raina P, *et al* (1998) *A Review of Therapies for Attention-Deficit Hyperactivity Disorder*. Ottawa: Canadian Co-Ordinating Office for Health Technology Assessment (CCOHTA).

Oosterlaan J, Logan G D & Sergeant J A (1998) **Response inhibition in AD/HD, CD, Comorbid AD/HD+CD, anxious, and control children: a meta-analysis of studies with the stop task**. *Journal of Child Psychology and Psychiatry and Allied Disciplines*, **39**, 411–425.

Silva R R, Munoz D M & Alpert M (1996) **Carbamazepine use in children and adolescents with features of attention-deficit hyperactivity disorder: a meta-analysis**. *Journal of the American Academy of Child and Adolescent Psychiatry*, **35**, 352–358.

Stein M A, Krasowski M, Leventhal B L, *et al* (1996) **Behavioral and cognitive effects of methylzanthines: a meta-analysis of theophylline and caffeine**. *Archives of Pediatrics and Adolescent Medicine*, **150**, 284–288.

Thurber S & Walker C E (1983) **Medication and hyperactivity: a meta-analysis**. *Journal of General Psychology*, **108**, 79–86.

Clinical guidelines

American Academy of Child and Adolescent Psychiatry (1997) **Practice parameters for the assessment and treatment of children, adolescents and adults with attention-deficit hyperactivity disorder**. *Journal of American Academy of Child Adolescent Psychiatry*, **36** (suppl.), 85S–121S.

Mental Health Committee of the Canadian Pediatric Society(1990) **The use of methylphenidate for attention–deficit hyperactivity disorder**. *Canadian Medical Association Journal*, **142**, 817–818.

Taylor E, Sergeant J, Doepfner M, *et al* (1998) **European guidelines: clinical guidelines for ADHD**. *Journal of European Child and Adolescent Psychiatry*, **7**, 184–200.

Reviews

Cantwell D (1996) **Attention deficit disorder: A review of the past 10 years**. *Journal of the American Academy of Child and Adolescent Psychiatry*, **35**, 978–987.

Overmeyer S & Taylor E (1999) **Annotation: principles of treatment for hyperkinetic disorder: practical approaches for the UK**. *Journal of Child Psychology and Psychiatry*, **40**, 1147–1157.

Classic papers

Bradley C (1937) **The behaviour of children receiving benzedrine**. *American Journal of Orthopsychiatry*, **15**, 577–585.

Cutting edge papers

Greenhill L, Abikoff H, Arnold E, *et al* (1996) **Medication treatment strategies in the MTA study: Revelance to clinicians and researchers**. *Journal of the American Academy of Child and Adolescent Psychiatry*, **35**, 1304–1313.

MTA Cooperative Group (1999) **A 14-month randomised clinical trial of treatment strategies for attention-deficit/hyperactivity disorder**. *Archives of General Psychiatry*, **56**, 1073–1086.

—— (1999) **Moderators and mediators of treatment response for children with attention-deficit/hyperactivity disorder**. *Archives of General Psychiatry*, **56**, 1097–1099.

Taylor E (1999) **Developmental neuropsychopathology of attention deficit and impulsiveness**. *Development and Psychopathology*, **11**, 607–628.

Reports

Gilmore A, Best L & Milne R (1998) ***Methylphenidate in Children with Hyperactivity***. DEC Report 78. South and West Research and Development Directorate.

Joughin C & Zwi M (1999) ***FOCUS on the Use of Stimulants in Children with Attention-Deficit Hyperactivity Disorder: a Primary Evidence-Base Briefing***. London: Research Unit, Royal College of Psychiatrists.

Cochrane Controlled Trials Register
131 hits (keywords: ADHD AND child*)
146 hits (keywords: "attention deficit hyperactivity disorder" AND child*)

Cochrane Developmental, Psychosocial and Learning Problems Group
Contact: Ms Jane Dennis, Bristol, UK. e-mail: J.Dennis@bristol.ac.uk

BULLYING

Systematic reviews and meta-analyses

Hawker D S J & Boulton M J (2000) **Twenty years' research on peer victimization and psychosocial maladjustment: a meta-analytic review of cross sectional studies**. *Journal of Child Psychology and Psychiatry*, **44**, 441–455.

Classic papers

Dawkins J (1995) **Bullying in schools: doctors' responsibilities**. *British Medical Journal*, **310**, 274–275.

Olweus D (1994) **Annotation: bullying at school: basic facts and effects of a school based intervention program**. *Journal of Child Psychology and Psychiatry*, **7**, 1171–1190.

Rigby K & Slee P T (1993) **Dimensions of interpersonal relation among Australian school children and implications for psychological well–being**. *Journal of Social Psychology*, **133**, 33–42.

Slee P T (1994) **Situational and interpersonal correlates of anxiety associated with peer victimization**. *Child Psychiatry and Human Development*, **25**, 97–107.

—— (1995) **Peer victimization and its relationship to depression among Australian primary school students**. *Personality and Individual Differences*, **18**, 57–62.

—— & Rigby K (1993) **Australian school children's self–appraisal of interpersonal relations: the bullying experience**. *Child Psychiatry and Human Development*, **23**, 273–282.

—— & —— (1993) **The relationship of Eysenck's personality factors and self-esteem to bully/victim behaviour in Australian schoolboys**. *Personality and Individual Differences*, **14**, 371–373.

Cutting edge papers

Forero R, McLellan L, Rissel C, *et al* (1999) **Bullying behaviour and psychosocial health among school students in New South Wales, Australia: a cross-sectional survey**. *British Medical Journal*, **319**, 344–348.

Kaltiala-Heino R, Rimpela M, Marttunen M, *et al* (1999) **Bullying, depression, and suicidal ideation in Finnish adolescents: school survey**. *British Medical Journal*, **319**, 348–351.

Kumpulainen K, Rasanen E, Henttonem I, *et al* (1998) **Bullying and psychiatric symptoms among elementary school-age children**. *Child Abuse and Neglect*, **22**, 705–717.

Salmon G, James A & Smith D M (1998) **Bullying in schools: self-reported anxiety, depression and self-esteem in secondary school children**. *British Medical Journal*, **317**, 924–925.

Smith P K & Myron-Wilson R (1998) **Parenting and school bullying**. *Clinical Child Psychology and Psychiatry*, **3**, 405–417.

Williams K, Chambers M, Logan S, *et al* (1996) **Association of common health symptoms with bullying in primary school children**. *British Medical Journal*, **313**, 17–19.

Books

Olweus D (1993) *Bullying in Schools: What We Know and What We Can Do*. Oxford: Blackwell.

Rigby K (1996) *Bullying in Schools and What to Do About it*. Melbourne: Australian Council for Educational Research.

Skinner A (1996) *Bullying: An Annotated Bibliography of Literature and Resources* (2nd edn). Leicester: Youth Work Press.

Smith P K & Sharp S (eds) (1994) *School Bullying: Insights and Perspectives*. London: Routledge.

Tattum, D P & Lane D A (eds)(1989) *Bullying in Schools*. Stoke on Trent: Trentham Books.

Cochrane Controlled Trials Register
1 hit (keywords: bully*)

Cochrane Developmental, Psychosocial and Learning Problems Group
Contact: Ms Jane Dennis, Bristol, UK. e-mail: J.Dennis@bristol.ac.uk

CONDUCT DISORDER: disruptive/aggressive behaviour

Systematic reviews and meta-analyses

Barlow J (1997) *Systematic Review of the Effectiveness of Parent Training Programmes in Improving Behavioural Problems in Children Aged 3–10 Years*. Oxford: Department of Public Health, Health Services Research Unit.

Dush D M, Hirt M L & Schroeder H E (1989) **Self-statement modification in the treatment of child behaviour disorders: a meta-analysis**. *Psychological Bulletin*, **106**, 97–106.

Kavale K A, Mathur S R, Forness S R, *et al* (1997) **Effectiveness of social skills training for students with behaviour disorders: a meta-analysis**. *Advances in Learning and Behavioural Disabilities*, **11**, 1–26.

Frick P J, Lahey B B, Loeber R, *et al* (1993) **Oppositional defiant disorder and conduct disorder: a meta-analytic review of factor analyses and cross-validation in a clinic sample**. *Clinical Psychology Review*, **13**, 319–340.

Griffiths M (1999) **Violent video games and aggression: a review of the literature**. *Aggression and Violent Behaviour*, **4**, 203–212.

Lipsey M (1992) **Juvenile deliquency treatment: a meta-analytic inquiry into the variability of effects**. In *Meta-Analysis for Explanation: a Casebook* (eds T D Cook, H Cooper, D S Cordray, *et al*), pp. 83–128. Thousand Oaks, CA: Russell Sage Foundation.

Loeber R & Schmaling K B (1985) **Empirical evidence for overt and covert patterns of antisocial conduct problems: a meta-analysis**. *Journal of Abnormal Child Psychology*, **13**, 337–353.

Miller P A & Eisenberg N (1988) **The relation of empathy to aggressive and externalizing/antisocial behaviour**. *Psychological Bulletin*, **103**, 324–344.

Serketich W J & Dumas J E (1996) **The effectiveness of behavioural parent training to modify antisocial behaviour in children: a meta-analysis**. *Behaviour Therapy*, **27**, 171–186.

Weaver T L & Clum G A (1995) **Psychological distress associated with interpersonal violence: a meta-analysis**. *Clinical Psychology Review*, **15**, 115–140.

Zoccolillo M (1992) **Co-occurrence of conduct disorder and its adult outcomes with depressive and anxiety disorders: a review**. *Journal of the American Academy of Child and Adolescent Psychiatry*, **31**, 547–556.

Clinical guidelines

American Academy of Child and Adolescent Psychiatry (1997) **Practice parameters for the assessment and treatment of children and adolescents with conduct disorder**. *Journal of the American Academy of Child and Adolescent Psychiatry*, **36** (suppl.), 122S–139S.

Webster-Stratton C (1993) **Strategies for helping early school-aged children with oppositional defiant and conduct disorders: the importance of home–school partnerships**. *School Psychology Review*, **22**, 437–457.

Reviews

Kazdin A E (1997) **Practitioner review: psychological treatments for conduct disorder in children**. *Journal of Child Psychology and Psychiatry*, **38**, 161–178.

—— (1998) **Current progress and future plans for developing effective treatments: comments and perspectives**. *Journal of Clinical Child Psychology*, **27**, 217–226.

Loeber R & Southomer-Loeber M (1986) **Family factors as correlates and predicators of juvenile conduct problems and delinquency**. In *Crime and Justice* (eds M. Tonry & N Morris), pp. 29–149. Chicago: University of Chicago Press.

Sheldrick C (1999) **Practitioner review: the assessment and management of risk in adolescents**. *Journal of Child Psychology and Psychiatry*, **40**, 507–518.

Utting D, Bright J & Henricson C (1993) **Crime and the Family**. London: Family Policy Studies Centre.

Webster-Stratton C (1997) **Treating children with early-onset conduct problems: a comparison of child and parent training interventions**. *Journal of Consulting and Clinical Psychology*, **65**, 93–109.

——, Hollingsworth T & Kolpacoff M (1989) **The long-term effectiveness and clinical significance of three cost-effective training programs for families with conduct-problem children**. *Journal of Consulting and Clinical Psychology*, **57**, 550–553.

Classic papers

Loeber R (1991) **Antisocial behaviour: more enduring than changeable?** *Journal of the American Academy of Child and Adolescent Psychiatry*, **30**, 393–397.

Patterson G R, Chamberlain P A & Reid J B (1982) **A comparative evaluation of a parent-training program**. *Behaviour Therapy*, **13**, 638–650.

Robins L N (1978) **Sturdy childhood predictors of adult antisocial behavior: replications from the longitudinal studies**. *Psychological Medicine*, **8**, 611–622.

Cutting edge papers

Lahey B B, Waldman I D & McBurnett K (1999) **Annotation: the development of antisocial behaviour: an integrative causal model**. *Journal of Child Psychology and Psychiatry*, **40**, 669–682.

Books

Kazdin A (1985) *Treatment of Antisocial Behaviour in Children and Adolescents*. Homewood, IL: Dorsey.

Cochrane Controlled Trials Register

46 hits (keywords: "conduct disorder")

64 hits (key words: "conduct disorder*")

26 hits (key words: "aggressive behaviour")

99 hits (key words: "aggressive behavior")

28 hits (key words: "aggressive behavior" AND child*)

Cochrane Developmental, Psychosocial and Learning Problems Group
Contact: Ms Jane Dennis, Bristol, UK. E-mail: J.Dennis@bristol.ac.uk

CONDUCT DISORDER: juvenile delinquency

Systematic reviews and meta-analyses

Nelson J R, Smith D J & Dodd J (1990) **The moral reasoning of juvenile delinquents: a meta-analysis**. *Journal of Abnormal Child Psychology*, **18**, 231–239.

Weaver T L & Clum G A (1995) **Psychological distress associated with interpersonal violence: a meta-analysis**. *Clinical Psychology Review*, **15**, 115–140.

Whitehead J T & Lab S P (1989) **A meta-analysis of juvenile correctional treatment**. *Journal of Research in Crime and Delinquency*, **26**, 276–295.

Reviews

Drewett A & Shepperdson B (1995) *A Literature Review of Services for Mentally Disordered Offenders*. LH37 10/95 AD.BS. Pp. 1–57. Leicester: Nuffield Community Care Studies Unit.

Greenwood P W (1996) **Responding to juvenile crime: lessons learned**. *Future of Children*, **6**, 75–85.

Snyder H N (1996) **The Juvenile Court and delinquency cases**. *Future of Children*, **6**, 53–63.

Classic papers

Farrington D P (1995) **The development of offending and antisocial behaviour from childhood: key findings from the Cambridge study in delinquent development**. *Journal of Child Psychology and Psychiatry*, **36**, 29–64.

Cochrane Developmental, Psychosocial and Learning Problems Group
Contact: Ms Jane Dennis, Bristol, UK. e-mail: J.Dennis@bristol.ac.uk

CONSULTATION

Clinical guidelines

Steinberg D (1985) **Consultative work in child and adolescent psychiatry**. In *Managing Children with Psychiatric Problems* (ed. M E Garradda), pp. 115–125. London: British Medical Journal Publishing Group.

—— (1992) **Informed consent: consultation and basis for collaboration between disciplines and between professionals and their patients**. *Journal of Interprofessional Care*, **6**, 43–48.

Reviews

Steinberg D (2000) **The child psychiatrist as consultant to schools and colleges**. In *New Oxford Textbook of Psychiatry* (eds M G Gelder, J J Lopez–Ibor & N C Andreason). Oxford: Oxford University Press.

—— & Yule W (1985) **Consultative work**. In *Child and Adolescent Psychiatry: Modern Approaches* (eds M Rutter & L Hersov), pp. 914–926 (2nd edn). Oxford: Blackwell Scientific Publications.

Classic papers

Menzies I E P (1988) *Selected Essays: Containing Anxiety in Institutions*. London: Free Association Books.

Books

Caplan G (1970) *The Theory and Practice of Mental Health Consultation*. London: Tavistock.

Gallescih J (1982) *The Profession and Practice of Consultation: A Handbook for Consultants, Trainers of Consultants and Consumers of Consultation Services*. London: Jossey–Bass.

Steinberg D (1989) *Interprofessional Consultation: Innovation and Imagination in Working Relationships*. Oxford: Blackwell Scientific Publications.

DELIBERATE SELF-HARM

Systematic reviews and meta-analyses

Chance S E, Kaslow N J, Summerville M B, *et al* (1998) **Suicidal behavior in African American individuals: current status and future directions**. *Cultural Diversity and Mental Health*, **4**, 19–37.

Hawton K, Arensman E, Townsend E, *et al* (1998) **Deliberate self-harm: systematic review of efficacy of psychosocial and pharmacological treatments in preventing repetition**. *British Medical Journal*, **317**, 441–447.

Van der Sande R, Buskens E, Allart E, *et al* (1997) **Psychosocial intervention following suicide attempt: a systematic review of treatment interventions**. *Acta Psychiatrica Scandinavica*, **96**, 43–50.

Clinical guidelines

Schmidtke A, Bille-Brahe U, Deleo D, *et al* (1996) **Attempted suicide in Europe: rates, trends, and socio-demographic characteristics of suicide attempters during the periods1989–1992. Results of the WHO/EURO Multi-Centre Study on Parasuicide**. *Acta Psychiatrica Scandinavica*, **93**, 327–338.

Reviews

Shaffer D & Piacentini J (1994) **Suicide and Attempted Suicide**. In *Child and Adolescent Psychiatry: Modern Approaches* (eds M Rutter, E Taylor & L Hersov), pp. 407–424. Oxford: Blackwell Scientific Publications.

Classic papers

Centers for Disease Control (1991) **Attempted suicide among high school students – United States**. *Morbidity and Mortality Weekly Report*, **40**, 633–635.

Shaffer D (1974) **Suicide in childhood and early adolescence**. *Journal of Child Psychology and Psychiatry*, **15**, 275–291.

——, Gould M, Fisher P, *et al* (1996) **Psychiatric diagnosis in child and adolescent suicide**. *Archives of General Psychiatry*, **53**, 339–348.

Reports

NHS Health Advisory Service (1994) *Suicide Prevention – the Challenge Confronted*. London: HMSO.

Royal College of Psychiatrists (1994) *Consensus Guidelines on the General Hospital Management of Deliberate Self-Harm Patients*. London: Royal College of Psychiatrists.

—— (1998) *Managing Deliberate Self-Harm in Young People*. Council Report CR64. London: Royal College of Psychiatrists.

New research and theories

Dicker R, Morrisey R F, Abikoff H *et al* (1997) **Hospitalizing the suicidal adolescent: decision-making criteria of psychiatric residents**. *Journal of the American Academy of Child and Adolescent Psychiatry*, **36**, 769–776.

Fombonne E (1998) **Suicidal behaviour in vulnerable adolescents. Time trends and their correlates**. *British Journal of Psychiatry*, **173**, 154–159.

Harrington R, Kerfoot M, Dyer E, *et al* (1998) **Randomised trial of family intervention for children who have deliberately poisoned themselves**. *Journal of the American Academy of Child and Adolescent Psychiatry*, **37**, 512–518.

Negron R, Piacentini J, Graae F, *et al* (1997) **Microanalysis of adolescent suicide attempters and ideators during the acute suicide episode**. *Journal of the American Academy of Child and Adolescent Psychiatry*, **36**,1512–1519.

Peterson B S, Zhang H, Santa Lucia R, *et al* (1996) **Risk factors for presenting problems in child psychiatric emergencies**. *Journal of the American Academy of Child and Adolescent Psychiatry*, **35**,1162–1173.

Shaffer D, Gould M S, Fisher P, *et al* (1996) **Psychiatric diagnosis in child and adolescent suicide**. *Archives of General Psychiatry*, **53**, 339–348.

Stein D L, Aptel A, Ratzoni G, *et al* (1998) **Association between multiple suicide attempts and negative affects in adolescents**. *Journal of the American Academy of Child and Adolescent Psychiatry*, **37**, 488–494.

Cochrane Controlled Trials Register
3 hits (keywords: "self harm" AND child*)
5 hits (keywords: "self harm" AND adolesc*)
20 hits (keywords: suicid* AND child*)

Cochrane Depression, Anxiety and Neurosis Group
Contact: Review Group Coordinator: Miss Natalie Khin, New Zealand;
e-mail: n.khin@auckland.ac.nz

EATING DISORDERS

Systematic reviews and meta-analyses

Allison D B & Faith M S (1996) **Hypnosis as an adjunct to cognitive–behavioural psychotherapy: a meta-analytic reappraisal**. *Journal of Consulting and Clinical Psychology*, **64**, 513–516. Reviewed on DARE.

Bacaltchuk J & Hay P (1999) **Pharmacotherapy for people with bulimia nervosa**. Protocol for a Cochrane Review. In *The Cochrane Library*. Issue 1. Oxford: Update Software.

Campbell K, Waters E, O'Meara S, *et al* (1999) **Interventions for preventing obesity in children**. Protocol for a Cochrane Review. In *The Cochrane Library*. Issue 4. Oxford: Update Software.

——, Summerbell C, O'Meara S, *et al* (1999) **Interventions for treating obesity in children**. Protocol for a Cochrane Review. In *The Cochrane Library*. Issue 4. Oxford: Update Software.

Epstein L H, Cloeman K J & Myers M D (1996) **Exercise in treating obesity in children and adolescents**. *Medicine and Science in Sports and Exercise*, **28,** 428–435. Reviewed on DARE.

Fombonne E (1995) **Anorexia nervosa. No evidence of an increase**. *British Journal of Psychiatry*, **166**, 462–471.

Glenny A M & O'Meara S (1997) **Systematic review of interventions in the treatment and prevention of obesity**. *CRD Report*, **10**, 1–149. Reviewed on DARE.

——, Melville A, O'Meara S, *et al* (1997) **The treatment and prevention of obesity: a systematic review of the literature**. *International Journal of Obesity and Related Metabolic Disorders*, **21**, 715–737.

Harvey E L, Glenny A, Kirk S F L, *et al* (1999) **Improving health professionals' management and the organization of care for overweight people**. Cochrane Review. In *The Cochrane Library*. Issue 1. Oxford: Update Software.

Hay P (1999) **Psychotherapy for binge eating disorder, purging and non-purging bulimia nervosa and related EDNOS syndromes**. Protocol for a Cochrane Review. In *The Cochrane Library*. Issue 1. Oxford: Update Software.

Kirsh I (1996) **Hypnotic enhancement of cognitive–behavioural weight loss treatments – another meta-reanalysis**. *Journal of Consulting and Clinical Psychology*, **64**, 517–519.

——, Montgomery G & Sapirstein G (1995) **Hypnosis as an adjunct to cognitive–behavioural psychotherapy: a meta-analysis**. *Journal of Consulting and Clinical Psychology*, **63**, 214–220. Reviewed on DARE.

Murnen S K & Smolak L (1997) **Femininity, masculinity, and disordered eating: a meta-analytic review**. *International Journal of Eating Disorders*, **22**, 231–242.

Schoemaker C (1997) **Does early intervention improve the prognosis in anorexia nervosa – a systematic review of the treatment-outcome literature**. *International Journal of Eating Disorders*, **21**, 1–15. Reviewed on DARE.

Wonderlich S A, Brewerton T D, Jocic J, *et al* (1997) **Relationship of childhood sexual abuse and eating disorders**. *Journal of the American Academy of Child and Adolescent Psychiatry*, **36**, 1107–1115.

Clinical guidelines

American Psychiatric Association (1993) **Practice guidelines for eating disorders**. *American Journal of Psychiatry*, **150**, 207–228.

Reviews

Lask B & Bryant-Waugh R (1995) **Eating disorders in children**. *Journal of Child Psychology and Psychiatry*, **36**, 191–202.

Steiner H & Lock J (1998) **Anorexia nervosa and bulimia nervosa in children and adolescents: a review of the past 10 years**. *Journal of the American Academy of Child and Adolescent Psychiatry*, **37**, 352–359.

Steinhausen H C (1997) **Annotation: outcome of anorexia nervosa in the younger patient**. *Journal of Child Psychology and Psychiatry*, **38**, 271–276.

Classic papers

Katzman D & Zipursky R (1997) **Adolescents with anorexia nervosa: the impact of the disorder on bones and brains**. Adolescent Nutritional Disorders Prevention and Treatment. *Annals of the New York Academy of Sciences*, **817**, 127–133.

Russell G F (1985) **Premenarchal anorexia nervosa and its sequelea**. *Journal of Psychiatric Research*, **19**, 363–369.

——,Smzukler G I, Dare C, *et al* (1987) **An evaluation of family therapy in anorexia nervosa and bulimia nervosa**. *Archives of General Psychiatry*, **44**, 1047–1056.

Cutting edge papers

Eisler I, Dare C, Russell G F, *et al* (1997) **Family and individual therapy in anorexia nervosa: a five–year follow–up**. *Archives of General Psychiatry*, **54**, 1025–1030.

Gordon, I (1997) **Anorexia nervosa in children: evidence of primary limbic abnormality**. *International Journal of Eating Disorders*, **22**, 159–165.

Reports

NHS Centre for Reviews and Dissemination (1997) **The prevention and treatment of obesity**. *Effective Health Care*, **3**, 1–12.

Office of Health Economics (1994) *Eating Disorders*. London: Office of Health Economics.

Books

Freeman C P & Newton J R (1992) **Anorexia nervosa: what treatments are most effective?** In *Practical Problems in Psychiatry* (eds K Hanton & P Cowen), pp. 77–92. Oxford: Oxford University Press.

Lask B & Bryant-Waugh R (1993) *Childhood Onset Anorexia Nervosa and Related Eating Disorders*. Sussex: Lawrence Erlbaum Associates.

ELIMINATION

Systematic reviews and meta-analyses

Lister-Sharp D, O'Meara S, Bradley M, *et al* (1997) *A Systematic Review of the Effectiveness of Interventions for Managing Childhood Nocturnal Enuresis*. CRD Report 11. York: University of York NHS Centre for Reviews and Dissemination.

Clinical guidelines

Felt B, Wise C G, Olson A, *et al* (1999) **Guideline for the management of paediatric idiopathic constipation and soiling**. *Archives of Paediatric and Adolescent Medicine*, **153,** 380–385.

Reviews

Butler R J (1998) **Annotation: night wetting in children: Psychological aspects**. *Journal of Child Psychology and Psychiatry*, **39**, 453–463.

Clayden G S (1992) **Management of chronic constipation**. *Archives of Disease in Childhood*, **67**, 340–344.

Kelly C P (1996) **Chronic constipation and soiling: a review of the psychological and family literature**. *Child Psychology and Psychiatry Review*, **1**, 59–66.

Levine M D & Backow H (1976) **Children with encopresis: a study of treatment outcome**. *Pediatrics*, **58**, 845–897.

Von Gontard A (1998) **Day and night wetting in children – a paediatric and child psychiatry perspective**. *Journal of Child Psychology and Psychiatry*, **39**, 439–451.

Classic papers

Anthony E J (1957) **An experimental approach to the psychopathology of childhood: encopresis**. *British Journal of Medical Psychology*, **30**, 146–175.

Berg I, Forsyth I, Holt P, *et al* (1982) **A controlled trial of 'Senokot' in faecal soiling treated with behavioural methods**. *Journal of Child Psychology and Psychiatry*, **149**, 543–549.

Levine M D (1975) **Children with encopresis: a descriptive analysis**. *Pediatrics*, **56**, 412–416.

White M (1984) **Pseudo-encopresis: from avalanche to victory, from vicious to virtuous cycles**. *Family Systems Medicine*, **2**, 150–160.

Cutting edge papers

Cox D J, Borowitz S, Kovatchev B, *et al* (1998) **Contributions of behaviour therapy and biofeedback to laxative therapy in the treatment of paediatric encopresis**. *Annals of Behavioural Medicine*, **20**, 70–76.

Stark L J, Opipari L C, Donaldson D L, *et al* (1997) **Evaluation of a standard protocol for retentive encopresis: a replication**. *Journal of Pediatric Psychology*, **22**, 619–633.

Cochrane Controlled Trials Register
16 hits (keywords: encopresis AND child*)
176 hits (keywords: enuresis AND child*)

Cochrane Developmental, Psychosocial and Learning Problems Group
Contact: Ms Jane Dennis, Bristol, UK. e-mail: J.Dennis@bristol.ac.uk

EMOTIONAL DISORDERS: anxiety and phobia

Systematic reviews and meta-analyses

Allen A J, Leonard H & Swedo S E (1995) **Current knowledge of medications for treatment of childhood anxiety disorders**. *Journal of the American Academy of Child and Adolescent Psychiatry*, **34**, 976–986.

Gammans R E, Stringfellow J C, Hvizdos, A J, *et al* (1992) **Use of busprione in patients with generalized anxiety disorder and coexisting depressive symptoms. A meta-analysis of eight randomized, controlled studies**. *Neuropsychobiology*, **25**, 193–201.

Gerlsman C, Emmelkamp P M & Arrindell W A (1990) **Anxiety, depression, and perception of early parenting: a meta-analysis**. *Clinical Psychology Review*, **10**, 251–277. (Erratum in **11**, 667).

Clinical guidelines

American Academy of Child and Adolescent Psychiatry (1997) **Practice parameters for the assessment and treatment of children with anxiety disorders**. *Journal of American Academy of Child and Adolescent Psychiatry*, **36** (suppl.), 69S–84S.

Reviews

Bernstein G A, Borchardt C M & Perwien A R (1996) **Anxiety disorders in children and adolescents: a review of the past ten years**. *Journal of the American Academy of Child and Adolescent Psychiatry*, **35**, 1110–1119.

Classic papers

Barlow D H, Cohen A S, Waddel M, *et al* (1984) **Panic and generalized anxiety disorders: nature and treatment**. *Behavior Therapy*, **15**, 431–449.

Graziano A M & Mooney K C (1982) **Behavioural treatment of 'nightfears' in children: maintenance of improvement at 2½–3 year follow-up**. *Journal of Consulting Clinical Psychology*, **50**, 598–599.

Cutting edge papers

Barrett P M, Dadds M R & Rapee R M (1996) **Family treatment of childhood anxiety: a controlled trial**. *Journal of Consulting and Clinical Psychology*, **64**, 333–342.

Kendall P C, Flannery-Schroeder E, Panichelli-Mindel S M, *et al* (1997) **Therapy for youths with anxiety disorders: a second randomized clinical trial**. *Journal of Consulting and Clinical Psychology*, **65**, 366–380.

King N J & Ollendick T H (1997) **Annotation: treatment of childhood phobias**. *Journal of Child Psychology and Psychiatry*, **38**, 389–400.

Books

Husain S A & Kashani J H (1992) ***Anxiety Disorders in Children and Adolescents***. Washington, DC: American Psychiatric Press.

Cochrane Controlled Trials Register
13 hits (keywords: phobia* AND child*)
11 hits (keywords: child* AND anxiety disorder*)

Cochrane Depression, Anxiety and Neurosis Group
Contact: Review Group Coordinator: Miss Natalie Khin, New Zealand;
e-mail: n.khin@auckland.ac.nz

EMOTIONAL DISORDERS: depression

Systematic reviews and meta-analyses

Bennett D S (1994) **Depression among children with chronic medical problems: a meta-analysis**. *Journal of Paediatric Psychology*, **19**, 149–169.

Gladstone T R & Kaslow N J (1995) **Depression and attributions in children and adolescents: a meta-analysis**. *Journal of Abnormal Child Psychology*, **23**, 597–606.

Harrington R, Whittaker J, Shoebridge P, *et al* (1998) **Systematic review of efficacy of cognitive behaviour therapies in child and adolescent depressive disorder**. *British Medical Journal*, **316**, 1559–1563.

Hazell P, O'Connell D, Heathcote D, *et al* (1995) **Efficacy of tricyclic drugs in treating child and adolescent depression: a meta-analysis**. *British Medical Journal*, **310**, 897–901.

Lapalme M, Hodgins S & LaRoche C (1997) **Children of parents with bipolar disorder: a meta-analysis of risk for mental disorders**. *Canadian Journal of Psychiatry*, **42**, 623–631.

Patten S B (1991) **The loss of a parent during childhood as a risk factor for depression**. *Canadian Journal of Psychiatry*, **36**, 706–711.

Reinecke M A, Ryan N E & Dubois D L (1998) **Cognitive–behavioural therapy of depression and depressive symptoms during adolescence: a review and meta-analysis**. *Journal of the American Academy of Child and Adolescent Psychiatry*, **37**, 26–34.

Thurber S, Ensign J, Punnett A F, *et al* (1995) **A meta-analysis of antidepressant outcome studies that involved children and adolescents**. *Journal of Clinical Psychology*, **51**, 340–345.

Clinical guidelines

American Academy of Child and Adolescent Psychiatry (1998) **Practice parameters for the assessment and treatment of children and adolescents with depressive disorders**. *Journal of the American Academy of Child and Adolescent Psychiatry*, **37** (suppl.) 63S–83S.

Reviews

Devane C L & Sallee F R (1996) **Serotonin selective reuptake inhibitors in child and adolescent psychopharmacology. A review of published experience**. *Journal of Clinical Psychiatry*, **57**, 55–66.

Harrington R, Whittaker J & Shoebridge P (1998) **Psychological treatment of depression in children and adolescents. A review of treatment research**. *British Journal of Psychiatry*, **173**, 291–298.

Classic papers

Harrington R, Fudge H, Rutter M, *et al* (1990) **Adult outcomes of childhood and adolescent depression: psychiatric status**. *Archives of General Psychiatry*, **47**, 465–473.

Puig-Antich J, Lukens E, Davies M, *et al* (1985) **Psychosocial functioning in prepubertal major depressive disorders. Interpersonal relationships during the depressive episode**. *Archives of General Psychiatry*, **42**, 500–507.

——, Perel J M, Lupatkin W, *et al* (1987) **Imipramine in prepubertal major depressive disorders**. *Archives of General Psychiatry*, **44**, 81–89.

Rutter M (1986) **The developmental psychopathology of depression: issues and perspectives**. In *Depression in Young People: Developmental and Clinical Perspectives* (eds M Rutter C Izard & P Read), pp. 3–30. New York: Guildford Press.

Ryan N D, Puig–Antich J, Ambrosini P, *et al* (1987) **The clinical picture of major depression in children and adolescents**. *Archives of General Psychiatry*, **44**, 854–861.

Cutting edge papers

Angold A, Costello E, Erkanli A, *et al* (1999) **Pubertal changes in hormone levels and depression in girls**. *Psychological Medicine*, **29**, 1043–1053.

Brent D, Holder D, Kolko D, *et al* (1997) **A clinical psychotherapy trial for adolescent depression comparing cognitive, family and supportive treatments**. *Archives of General Psychiatry*, **54**, 877–885.

Emslie G, Rush A, Weinberg W, *et al* (1997) **A double-blind, randomized placebo-controlled trial of fluoxetine in depressed children and adolescents**. *Archives of General Psychiatry*, **54**, 1031–1037.

Goodyer I M, Herbert J, Secher S M, *et al* (1997) **Short-term outcome of major depression: comorbidity and severity at presentation as predictors of persistent disorder**. *Journal of the American Academy of Child and Adolescent Psychiatry*, **36**, 179–187.

Hankin B L, Abramson L Y, Moffitt T E, *et al* (1998) **Development of depression from preadolescence to young adulthood: emerging gender differences in a 10-year longitudinal study**. *Journal of Abnormal Psychology*, **107**, 128–140.

Strober M, Rao U, De Antonio M, *et al* (1998) **Effects of electroconvulsive therapy in adolescents with severe endogenous depression resistant to pharmacotherapy**. *Biological Psychiatry*, **43**, 335–338.

Books

Goodyer I (ed.) (1995) *The Depressed Child and Adolescent. Developmental and Clinical Perspectives*. Cambridge: Cambridge University Press.

Harrington R C (1993) *Depressive Disorder in Childhood and Adolescence*. Chichester: Wiley.

Other

Aisher A J (1999) **Mood disorder in suicidal children and adolescents: recent developments**. *Journal of Child Psychology and Psychiatry*, **40**, 315–324.

Churchill R. & Gill D (1996) **Drug treatment of childhood depression**. *Bandolier*, **3**, 29–37.

Cochrane Controlled Trials Register
6 hits (keywords: "childhood depression")
75 hits (keywords: "depressive disorder*" AND child*)
8771 hits (keywords: "depressive disorder*" AND adolescen*)

Cochrane Depression, Anxiety and Neurosis Group
Contact: Review Group Coordinator: Miss Natalie Khin, New Zealand;
e-mail: n.khin@auckland.ac.nz

Systematic reviews and meta-analyses

Geller D, Biederman J, Jones J, *et al* (1998) **Is juvenile obsessive–compulsive disorder: a developmental subtype of the disorder? A review of the paediatric literature**. *Journal of the American Academy of Child and Adolescent Psychiatry*, **37**, 420–427.

Oakley-Browne M & Doughty C (1997) **Psychological and pharmacological treatments of obsessive–compulsive disorder**. Protocol for a Cochrane Review. In *The Cochrane Library*. Issue 1. Oxford: Update Software.

Piccinelli M, Pini S, Bellantuono C, *et al* (1995) **Efficacy of drug treatment in obsessive–compulsive disorder: a meta-analytic review**. *British Journal of Psychiatry*, **166**, 424–443.

Clinical guidelines

American Academy of Child and Adolescent Psychiatry (1998) **Practice parameters for the assessment and treatment of children and adolescents with obsessive–compulsive disorder**. *Journal of the American Academy of Child and Adolescent Psychiatry*, **37** (suppl.), 27S–42S.

March J & Mulle K (1998) *OCD in Children and Adolescents: a Cognitive Behavioural Treatment Manual*. New York: Guildford.

——, Frances A, Carpenter D, *et al* (1997) **The expert consensus guideline series: treatment of obsessive–compulsive disorder**. *Journal of Clinical Psychiatry*, **4** (suppl.), 2–72.

Reviews

Bolton D (1998) **Obsessive–compulsive disorder**. In *Comprehensive Clinical Psychology: Children and Adolescents* (vol. 5)(eds M Hersen & A Bellack), pp. 367–391. San Francisco, CA: Pergamon.

Francis G & Cragg R A (1996) *Childhood Obsessive–Compulsive Disorder*. Thousands Oaks, CA: Sage.

Heyman I (1997) **Children with obsessive–compulsive disorder**. *British Medical Journal*, **315**, 444.

Rapoport J L (ed.) (1989) *Obsessive–Compulsive Disorder in Children and Adolescents*. Washington, DC: American Psychiatric Press.

Classic papers

Bolton D, Collins S & Steinberg D (1983) **The treatment of obsessive–compulsive disorder in adolescence: a report of 15 cases**. *British Journal of Psychiatry*, **142**, 456–464.

Leonard H L, Swedo S E, Rapoport J L, *et al* (1989) **Treatment of obsessive–compulsive disorder with clomipramine and desipramine in children and adolescents**. *Archives of General Psychiatry*, **46**, 1088–1092.

Valleni-Basile L A, Garrison C Z, Jackson K L, *et al* (1994) **Frequency of obsessive–compulsive disorder in a community sample of young adolescents**. *Journal of the American Academy of Child and Adolescent Psychiatry*, **33**, 782–791.

(Cutting edge papers)

Bolton D (1996) **Annotation: developmental issues in obsessive compulsive disorder**. *Journal of Child Psychology and Psychiatry*, **37**, 131–137.

Evans D W, Leckman J F, Carter A, *et al* (1997) **Ritual, habit and perfectionism: the prevalence and development of compulsive-like behaviour in normal young children**. *Child Development*, **68**, 58–68.

Cochrane Controlled Trials Register
31 hits (keywords: "obsessive compulsive disorder" AND child*)
61 hits (keywords: "obsessive compulsive disorder" AND adolescence)
19 hits (keywords: "obsessive compulsive disorder" AND adolescent*)

GENDER IDENTITY DISORDERS

Systematic reviews

Di Ceglie D (1995) **Gender identity disorders in children and adolescents**. *British Journal of Hospital Medicine*, **53**, 251–256.

Scott Heller S (1997) **Gender identity disorder**. *The Signal – Newsletter of the World Association for Infant Mental Health*, **5**, 1–8.

Classic papers

Coates S, Friedman R C & Wolfe S (1991) **The aetiology of boyhood gender identity disorder: a model for integrating temperament development and psychodynamics**. *Psychoanalytic Dialogues*, **1**, 481–523.

Money J (1994) **The concept of gender identity in childhood and adolescence after 39 years**. *Journal of Sex and Marital Therapy*, **20**, 163–177.

Stoller R J (1992) **Gender identity development and prognosis: a summary**. In *New Approaches to Mental Health from Birth to Adolescence* (eds C Chiland & J G Young), pp. 78–87. New Haven & London: Yale University Press.

Cutting edge papers

Cohen-Kettenis P T & van Goozen S M M (1997) **Sex reassignment of adolescent transsexuals: a follow-up study**. *Journal of the American Academy of Child and Adolescent Psychiatry*, **36**, 263–271.

Di Ceglie D (1998) **Management and therapeutic aims in working with children and adolescents with gender identity disorders, and their families**. In *A Stranger in My Own Body – Atypical Gender Identity Development and Mental Health* (eds D De Ceglie & D Freedman), pp.185–197. London: Karnac Books.

Reports

Royal College of Psychiatrists (1998) *Gender Identity Disorders in Children and Adolescents: Guidance for Management*. Council Report CR63. London: Royal College of Psychiatrists.

Books

Di Ceglie D & Freedman D (1998) *A Stranger in My Own Body – Atypical Gender Identity Development and Mental Health*. London: Karnac Books.

Green R (1994) *Sexual Identity Conflicts in Children and Adolescents*. New York: Basic Books.

Zucker K J & Bradley S J (1995) *Gender Identity Disorders and Psychosexual Problems in Children and Adolescents*. New York: Guildford Press.

LEGAL ISSUES: consent and competence

The law

Gilick *v.* West Norfolk and Wisbech Area Health Authority [1986] *AC*, 112.

Kennedy I & Grubb A (1994) *Medical Law* (2nd edn). London: Butterworths.

Re: C. Adult: refusal of treatment [1994] **1**, *WLR*, 290.

Re: R. A minor: wardship: medical treatment [1992] Fam 11 [1991] 4, *All ER*, 177, CA.

Re: W. A minor: wardship: medical treatment [1993] Fam 64 [1992] 4, *All ER*, 627, CA.

White R, Car P & Lowe N (1995) *The Children Act in Practice*. London: Butterworths.

Williams R & White R (1996) *Safeguards for Young Minds*. Gaskell: London.

Guidelines

Alderson P & Montgomery J (1996) *Health Care Choices: Making Decisions with Children*. London: Institute of Public Policy Research.

British Medical Association & the Law Society (1995) *Assessment of Mental Capacity*. London: British Medical Association.

General Medical Council (1999) *Seeking Patient's Consent: the Ethical Considerations*. London: General Medical Council.

Pearce J (1994) **Consent to treatment during childhood: the assessment of competence and avoidance of conflict.** *British Journal of Psychiatry*, **165**, 713–716.

Shaw M (1999) *Treatment Decisions in Young People: the Legal Framework*. London: Research Unit, Royal College of Psychiatrists.

—— (1999) *Treatment Decisions in Young People: Clinical Guidelines*. London: Research Unit, Royal College of Psychiatrists.

—— (1999) *Treatment Decisions in Young People: Frequently Asked Questions and References*. London: College Research Unit.

Classic papers

Roth L, Meisel A & Lidz C (1977) **Test of competence to consent to treatment.** *American Journal of Psychiatry*, **134**, 279.

Shaw A (1973) **Dilemmas of 'informed consent' in children.** *New England Journal of Medicine*, **289**, 885–890.

Research

Alderson P (1993) *Children's Consent to Surgery*. Buckingham: Open University Press.

Rylance G, Bowen C & Rylance J (1995) **Measles and rubella immunisation: information and consent in children**. *British Medical Journal*, **311**, 923–924.

Weithorn L A & Campbell S B (1982) **The competency of children and adolescents to make informed treatment decisions**. *Child Development*, **53**, 1589–1599.

Practitioners' textbooks

Family Court Practice (1999) *Family Court Practice*. Bristol: Jordans.

Munro P & Forrester L (1999) *The Guardian ad Litem: Law and Practice* (2nd edn). Bristol: Jordans.

White R, Carr P & Lowe N (1995) *The Children Act in Practice*. London: Butterworths.

Guidance issued by the Department of Health

Department of Health (1990) *An Introduction to the Children Act 1989*. London: HMSO.

—— (1990) *The Care of Children – Principles and Practice in Regulations and Guidance*. London: HMSO.

—— (1991) *Court Orders. Children Act 1989 Guidance and Regulations* (vol.1, (grey book). London: HMSO.

—— (1991) *Family Support, Day Care and Educational Provision for Young Children. Children Act 1989 Guidance and Regulations* (vol. 2, blue book). London: HMSO.

—— (1991) *Family Placements. Children Act 1989 Guidance and Regulations* (vol. 3, orange book). London: HMSO.

—— (1991) *Residential Care. Children Act 1989 Guidance and Regulations* (vol. 4, yellow book). London: HMSO.

—— (1991) *Working Together*. London: HMSO.

Essential Department of Health publications

Department of Health (1989) *A Guide for Guardians ad Litem in Public Law Proceedings under the Children Act 1989*. London: Department of Health.

—— (1985) *Social Work Decisions in Child Care – Recent Research Findings and their Implications*. London: HMSO.

—— (1988) *Protecting Children – A Guide for Social Workers Undertaking a Comprehensive Assessment*. London: HMSO.

—— (1991) *Patterns and Outcomes and Child Placement: Messages from Current Research and their Implications*. London: HMSO.

—— (1993) *Memorandum of Good Practice: a Guide on Interviewing*. London: HMSO.

—— (1995) *Child Protection: Messages from Research*. London: The Stationery Office.

—— (1995) *The Challenge of Partnership in Child Protection: Practice Guide*. London: The Stationery Office.

—— (1996) *Avoiding Delay in Children Act Cases*. London: The Stationery Office.

—— (1996) *Reporting to Court under the Children Act*. London: The Stationery Office.

—— (1999) *Framework for the Assessment of Children in Need and their Families*. London: The Stationery Office.

Recommended reading

Adock M & White R (1998) *Significant Harm: its Management and Outcome*. Croydon: Significant Publications.

Children Act Advisory Committee (1997) *Children Act Advisory Committee Report (1996/1997)*. London: Family Policy Division, Lord Chancellors Department.

Hunt J & Macleod A (1998) *Statutory Intervention in Child Protection*. Bristol: University of Bristol.

King P & Young I (1992) *The Child as a Client: a Handbook for Solicitors who Represent Children*. Bristol: Family Law.

Lindley B (1994) *On the Receiving End: Families Experiences of the Court Process in Care and Supervision Proceedings under the Children Act 1989*. London: Family Rights Group.

Wilson K & James A (eds) (1995) *The Child Protection Handbook*. London: Bailliere-Tindall.

British Agencies for Adoption and Fostering publications

Address: Skyline House, 200 Union Street, London SE1 0LY; telephone: 020 7593 2072.

Batty D (1991) *Sexually Abused Children – Making Placements Work*. London: British Agencies for Adoption and Fostering.

—— (1993) *HIV Infection and Children in Need*. London: British Agencies for Adoption and Fostering.

—— & Cullen D (1996) *Child Protection. The Therapeutic Option*. London: British Agencies for Adoption and Fostering.

Chennells P & Hammond C (1998) *Adopting a Child*. London: British Agencies for Adoption and Fostering.

—— & Morrison M (1998) *Talking About Adoption*. London: British Agencies for Adoption and Fostering.

Falberg V (1994) *A Child's Journey Through Placement*. London: British Agencies for Adoption and Fostering.

Fratter J, Rowe J, Sapsford D, *et al* (1991) *Permanent Family Placement*. London: British Agencies for Adoption and Fostering.

Phillips R & McWilliam E (1996) *After Adoption. Working with Adoptive Families*. London: British Agencies for Adoption and Fostering.

Rushton A, Treseder J & Quinton D (1988) *New Parents for Older Children*. London: British Agencies for Adoption and Fostering.

Recommended periodicals

Adoption and Fostering. British Agency for Adoption and Fostering, 200 Union Street, London SE1 0lX.

Child and Family Law Quarterly. Jordan and Sons, 21 St Thomas Street, Bristol BS1 6JS.

Childright. Children's Legal Centre, PO Box 3314, London N1 2WA

Family Law. Jordan and Sons, 21 St Thomas Street, Bristol BS1 6JS.

Representing Children. National Youth Advocacy Service, 1 Downham Road, Heswell, Wirral CH60 5RG.

LEGAL ISSUES: parenting assessment

Systematic reviews and meta-analyses

None identified.

Clinical guidelines

Drummond D C & Fitzpatrick G (2000) **Children of substance misusing parents**. In *Family Matters: Interfaces Between Child and Adult Mental Health* (eds P Reder, M McClure & A Jolley), pp. 135–149. London: Routledge.

Jenner S (1997) **Assessment of parenting in the context of child protection using the Parent/Child Game**. *Child Psychology and Psychiatry Review*, **2**, 58–62.

Schuff G H & Asen K E (1996) **The disturbed parent and the disturbed family**. In *Parental Psychiatric Disorder: Distressed Parents and their Families* (eds M Gopfert, J Webster & M V Seeman), pp. 135–151. Cambridge: Cambridge University Press.

Reviews

Budd K S & Holdsworth M J (1996) **Issues in the clinical assessment of minimal parenting competence**. *Journal of Clinical Child Psychology*, **25**, 2–14.

Gopfert M, Webster J, Pollard J, *et al* (1996) **The assessment and prediction of parenting capacity: a community-oriented approach**. In *Parental Psychiatric Disorder: Distressed Parents and their Families* (eds M Gopfert, J Webster & M V Seeman), pp. 271–309. Cambridge: Cambridge University Press.

Mrazek D A, Mrazek P & Klinnert M (1995) **Clinical assessment of parenting**. *Journal of the American Academy of Child and Adolescent Psychiatry*, **34**, 272–282.

Reder P & Lucey C (eds) (1995) **Assessment of Parenting: Psychiatric and Psychological Contributions**. London: Routledge.

Classic papers

Kelmer-Pringle M (1978) **The needs of children**. In *The Maltreatment of Children* (ed. S M Smith), pp. 221–243. Lancaster: MTP Press.

Rutter M & Quinton D (1984) **Parental psychiatric disorder: effects on children**. *Psychological Medicine*, **14**, 853–880.

Swadi H (1994) **Parenting capacity and substance misuse: an assessment scheme**. *Association of Child Psychology and Psychiatry Review and Newsletter*, **16**, 237–244.

Cutting edge papers

Kumar R & Hipwell A E (1996) **Development of a clinical rating scale to assess mother–infant interaction in a psychiatric mother and baby unit**. *British Journal of Psychiatry*, **169**, 18–26.

Louis A, Condon J, Shute R, *et al* (1997) **The development of the Louis MACRO (mother and child risk observation) Forms: assessing parent–infant–child risk in the presence of maternal mental illness**. *Child Abuse and Neglect*, **21**, 589–606.

Reder P & Duncan S (1999) **Conflictual relationships and risks of child abuse**. *Journal of Child Centred Practice*, **6**, 127–145.

(**Books**)

Hagell A (1998) ***Dangerous Care: Reviewing the Risks to Children from their Carers***. London: Policy Studies Institute/The Bridge Child Care Development Service.

Herbert M (1996) ***Assessing Children in Need and their Parents***. Leicester: BPS Books.

Association of Directors of Social Services & Royal College of Psychiatrists (1995) *Joint Statement on an Integrated Mental Health Service for Children and Adolescents*. London: Royal College of Psychiatrists.

Audit Commission (1999) *Children in Mind: Child and Adolescent Mental Health Services*. London: Audit Commission.

Berger M, Hill P, Sein E, *et al* (1993) *A Proposed Core Data Set for Child and Adolescent Psychology and Psychiatry Services*. London: Association for Child Psychology and Psychiatry.

Bullock R, Gooch D & Little M (1999) *Children Going Home: the Reunification of Families*. Aldershot: Ashgate Publishing.

Chesson R & Chisholm D (eds) (1996) *Child Psychiatric Units at the Crossroads*. London: Jessica Kingsley.

Department of Education and Employment (1999) *Learning to Succeed: A New Framework for Post-16 Learning*. London: The Stationery Office.

—— (1999) *Sure Start: A Guide for Trailblazers*. London: The Stationery Office.

Department of Health (1996) *The Patient's Charter: Services for Children and Young People*. London: The Stationery Office.

—— (1998) *Children Looked After by Local Authorities: Government Response to the Second Report of the Health Committee on Children Looked After by Local Authorities: Session 1997–98*. London: The Stationery Office.

—— (1998) *Modernising Health and Social Services: National Priorities Guidance, 1999/00 – 2001–02*. Health Service Circular HSC(98)159, Local Authority Circular LAC(98)22. London: Department of Health.

—— (1998) *Families in Focus: Evaluation of the Department of Health's Refocusing Children's Services Initiative*. London: Department of Health.

—— (1998) *Someone Else's Children: Inspection of Planning and Decision-Making for Children Looked After and The Safety of Children Looked After*. London: Department of Health.

—— (1999) *Convention on the Rights of the Child: Second Report to the UN Committee on the Rights of the Child by the United Kingdom*. London: The Stationery Office.

—— (1999) *Consultation Draft Framework for the Assessment of Children in Need and their Families*. London: Department of Health.

—— (1999) *NHS Modernisation Fund and Mental Health Grants for Child and Adolescent Mental Health Services 1999/2000*. Health Service Circular HSC 1999/126; Local Authority Circular LAC(99)22. London: Department of Health.

—— (1999) *The Government's Objectives for Children's Social Services*. London: Department of Health.

Department of Health & Department for Education (1995) *A Handbook on Child and Adolescent Mental Health*. Manchester: The Stationery Office.

Department of Health, Home Office, Department for Education and Employment, *et al* (1991) *A Guide to Interagency Working to Safeguard and Promote the Welfare of Children – Consultation Draft*. London: Department of Health.

Finch J & Hill P (2000) *Health Advisory Service Standards for Child and Adolescent Mental Health Services*. Brighton: Pavillion Publishing.

Green J & Jacobs B (eds) (1998) *In-Patient Child Psychiatry*. London: Routledge.

Harrington R C, Kerfoot M, Veroluyn C, *et al* (1999) **Developing needs-led child and adult mental health services: issues and prospects**. *European Child and Adolescent Psychiatry*, **8**, 1–10.

House of Commons Health Committee (1998) *Children Looked After by Local Authorities: Session 1997–98*. Health Committee Second Report: Vol. 1. London: The Stationery Office.

House of Commons Select Health Committee (1997) *Inquiry into Mental Health Services*. London: HMSO.

Mental Health Foundation (1999) *Bright Futures: Promoting Children and Young People's Mental Health*. London: Mental Health Foundation.

NHS Executive (1998) *Information for Health: An Information Strategy for the Modern NHS 1998–2005: A National Stretegy for Local Implementation*. London: Department of Health.

Kurtz Z (ed.) (1992) *With Health in Mind: Mental Health Care for Children and Young People* (Quality Review Series). London: Action for Sick Children.

—— (1996) *Treating Children Well: A Guide to Using the Evidence Base in Commissioning and Managing Services for the Mental Health of Children and Young People*. London: The Mental Health Foundation.

——, Thornes R & Wolkind S (1996) *Services for the Mental Health of Children and Young People in England: a National Review. Report to the Department of Health*. London: South West Thames Regional Health Authority.

——, —— & —— (1996) *Services for the Mental Health of Children and Young People in England: Assessment of Needs and Unmet Need. Report to the Department of Health*. London: South West Thames Regional Health Authority.

Little M & Mount K (1999) *Prevention and Early Intervention with Children in Need*. Aldershot: Ashgate Publishing.

NACRO (1998) *Children, Schools and Crime: A Report by NACRO's Committee on Children and Crime (1998)*. London: NACRO.

NHS Executive (1996) *NHS Psychotherapy Services in England*. London: Department of Health.

NHS Health Advisory Service (1995) *Together We Stand: Thematic Review on the Commissioning, Role and Management of Child and Adolescent Mental Health Services*. London: The Stationery Office.

OFSTED (1999) *Principles into Practice: Effective Education for Pupils with Emotional and Behavioural Difficulties*. London: The Stationery Office.

Pearce J & Holmes S (1995) *Health Gain Investment Programme. Technical Review Document. People with Mental Health Problems (Part Four): Child and Adolescent Mental Health*. London: NHS Executive Trent and Centre for Mental Health Services Department.

Royal College of Psychiatrists (1999) *Guidance on Staffing of Child and Adolescent In-Patient Psychiatry Units*. Council Report CR76. London: Royal College of Psychiatrists.

Social Exclusion Unit, Home Office & Department of Health and Department for Education and Employment (1999) *School Inclusion: Pupil Support: The Secretary of State's Guidance on Pupil Attendance, Behaviour, Exclusion and Re-Integration*. Circular No. 10/99 and 11/99. London: Department of Health.

Social Services Inspectorate (1993–96) *Standards Used by the Social Services Inspectorate: Children's Services*. Vol. 2, pp. 146. London: Department of Health.

—— (1993–96) *Standards Used by the Social Services Inspectorate: Children's Residential Care, Secure Accommodation and Juvenile Justice*. Vol. 3, pp. 135. London: Department of Health.

Target M & Fonagy P (1996) **The psychological treatment of child and adolescent psychiatric disorders**. In *What Works for Whom?* (eds A Roth & P Fonagy). London: Guildford Press.

Utting W (1997) *People Like Us: the Report of the Review of the Safeguards for Children Living Away from Home*. London: Department of Health.

Wallace S A, Crown J M, Cox A D, *et al* (1997) **Epidemiologically based needs assessment: child and adolescent mental health**. In *Health Care Needs Assessment* (eds A Stevens & J Raftery). Oxford: Redcliffe Medical Press.

PAEDIATRIC LIAISON: chronic fatigue syndrome

Systematic reviews and meta-analyses

None identified.

Clinical guidelines

None identified.

Reviews

Richards J (2000) **Chronic fatigue syndrome in children and adolescents: a review article**. *Clinical Child Psychology and Psychiatry*, **5**, 31–51.

Classic papers

Bell K M, Cookfair D, Bell D S, *et al* (1991) **Risk factors associated with chronic fatigue syndrome in cluster of paediatric cases**. *Review of Infectious Diseases*, **13** (suppl.), 32S–38S.

Walford G A, Nelson W M & McCluskey D R (1993) **Fatigue, depression and social adjustment in chronic fatigue syndrome**. *Archives of Disease in Childhood*, **68**, 348–388.

Wessely S (1990) **Old wine in new bottles: neurasthenia and 'ME'**. *Psychological Medicine*, **20**, 35–53.

Cutting edge papers

Carter B, Edwards J, Kronenberger W, *et al* (1995) **Case control study of chronic fatigue in paediatric patients**. *Pediatrics*, **95**, 179–186.

Fox R (1998) ***A Research Portfolio on Chronic Fatigue***. London: The Royal Society of Medicine Press.

Fry A & Martin M (1996) **Cognitive idiosyncrasies among children with the chronic fatigue syndrome: anomalies in self–reported activity levels**. *Journal of Psychosomatic Research*, **41**, 213–223.

Plioplys A (1997) **Chronic fatigue syndrome should not be diagnosed in children**. *Pediatrics*, **100**, 270–271.

Reports

Anon (1997) ***Chronic Fatigue Syndrome: Report of the Committee of the Royal Colleges of Physicians, Psychiatrists and General Practioners***. London: Royal College of Physicians.

Best L & Stevens A (1996) ***Cognitive Behavioural Therapy in the Treatment of Chronic Fatigue Syndrome. Development and Evaluation Committee***. Report 50. Southampton: Wessex Institute for Health Research and Development.

Books

Marcovitch H (1991) **Chronic fatigue states in children**. In ***Post Viral Fatigue Syndrome*** (eds R Jenkins & J Mowbray), pp. 335–433. Chichester: John Wiley and Sons.

Taylor D (1992) **Outlandish factitious illness**. In *Recent Advances in Paediatrics* (ed. T David), pp. 63–76. Edinburgh: Churchill Livingstone.

Wessely S, Hotopf M & Sharpe M (1998) *Chronic Fatigue and its Syndromes*. Oxford: Oxford University Press.

Cochrane Controlled Trials Register
2 hits (keywords: chronic fatigue syndrome* AND child*)

Cochrane Depression, Anxiety and Neurosis Group
Contact: Review Group Coordinator: Miss Natalie Khin, New Zealand;
e–mail: n.khin@auckland.ac.nz

PAEDIATRIC LIAISON: dementia

Reviews

Goodman R (1994) **Brain disorders**. In *Child and Adolescent Psychiatry, Modern Approaches* (eds M Rutter, E Taylor & L Hersov), pp. 172–190. Oxford: Blackwell Scientific.

Rett syndrome

Reviews

Harris J C (1996) **Rett's disorder**. *Developmental Neuropsychiatry*, **2**, 228–238.

Cutting edge papers

Leonard H & Bower C (1998) **Is the girl with Rett syndrome normal at birth?** *Developmental Medicine and Child Neurology*, **40**, 115–121.

Disintegrative psychosis

Reviews

Harris J C (1996) **Childhood disintegrative disorder**. *Developmental Neuropsychiatry*, **2**, 239–243.

Cutting edge papers

Russo M, Perry R, Kolodny E, *et al* (1996) **Heller syndrome in a pre-school boy. Proposed medical evaluation and hypothesized pathogenesis.** *European Child and Adolescent Psychiatry*, **5**, 172–177.

Deterioration in autism

Reviews

Gillberg C & Schaumann H (1989) **Autism: specific problems of adolescence**. In *Diagnosis and Treatment of Autism* (ed. C Gillberg), pp. 375–382. New York and London: Plenum.

Down's syndrome

Johannsen P, Christensen J E & Mai J (1996) **The prevalence of dementia in Down syndrome**. *Dementia*, **7**, 221–225.

Zigman W B, Schupf N, Sersen E, *et al* (1996) **Prevalence of dementia in adults with and without Down syndrome**. *American Journal of Mental Retardation*, **100**, 403–412.

Reviews

Gascon C G (1996) **Subacute sclerosing panencephalitis**. *Seminars in Pediatric Neurology*, **3**, 260–269.

Cutting edge papers

Forrest G & Stores G (1996) **Subacute sclerosing panencephalitis presenting with psychosis and possible sexual abuse**. *European Child and Adolescent Psychiatry*, **5**, 110–113.

Papazian O, Canizales E, Alfonson I, *et al* (1995) **Reversible dementia and apparent brain atrophy during valporate therapy**. *Annals of Neurology*, **38**, 687–691.

Cochrane Controlled Trials Register
7 hits (keywords: "Rett syndrome")
3 hits (keywords: autism AND dementia)
2 hits (keywords: "down syndrome" AND dementia)
2 hits (keywords: "subacute sclerosing panencephalitis" AND child)

Cochrane Movement Disorders Group
Contact: Review Group Coordinator: Dr Joaquim Ferreire Lisbon, Portugal.
Tel: 351 1797 3453; e–mail: Movementdisord@mail.telepac.pt

PAEDIATRIC LIAISON: dying child

Reviews

Dyregrov A (1994) **Childhood bereavement consequences and therapeutic approaches**. *Association for Child Psychology and Psychiatry Review and Newsletter,* **16** (July), 173–183.

Harrington R & Harrison L (1999) **Unproven assumptions about the impact of bereavement on children**. *Journal of the Royal Society of Medicine,* **92**, 230–233.

Stambrook M & Parker K C H (1987) **The development of the concept of death in childhood. A review of the literature**. *Merrill Palmer Quarterly,* **33**, 133–157.

Classic papers

Bowlby J (1979) *The Making and Breaking of Affectional Bonds*. London: Tavistock.

Kane B (1967) **Children's concepts of death**. *Journal of Genetic Psychiatry,* **17**, 593–597.

General reading

Black D (1978) **The bereaved child**. *Journal of Child Psychology and Psychiatry,* **19**, 287–292.

Dyregrov A (1991) *Grief in Children. A Handbook for Adults*. London: Jessica Kingsley.

Earnshaw–Smith E (1982) **Emotional pain in dying patients and their families**. *Nursing Times,* **78**, 1865–1867.

Pettle S A & Britten C M (1995) **Talking with children about death and dying**. *Child: Care, Health and Development,* **21**, 395–404.

Death in the family

Ackworth A & Bruggen P (1985) **Family therapy when one member is on the death bed**. *Journal of Family Therapy,* **7**, 379–385.

Bisson J L & Cullum M (1994) **Group therapy for bereaved children**. *Association of Child Psychology and Psychiatry Review and Newsletter,* **16** (May), 130–139.

Krasner S & Beinart H (1989) **The Monday Group: a brief intervention with the siblings of infants who died from SIDS**. *Association of Child Psychology and Psychiatry Newsletter,* **11**, 11–17.

Masterman S H & Reams R (1988) **Support groups for bereaved pre-school and school age children**. *American Journal of Orthopsychiatry,* **58**, 562–570.

Smith S & Pennells M (1991) **Bereaved children and adolescents**. In *Groupwork with Children and Adolescents: A Handbook* (ed. K Dwivedi), pp. 195–208. London: Jessica Kingsley.

57

On more unusual situations

Harris-Hendricks J, Black D, Kaplan T, *et al* (1993) *When Father Kills Mother: Guiding Children Through Trauma and Grief*. London: Routledge.

Pettle S (1998) **Thinking about the future when death is inevitable: consultations in terminal care.** *Clinical Child Psychology and Psychiatry*, **3**, 131–139.

Udwin O (1993) **Children's reactions to trauma.** *Journal of Child Psychology and Psychiatry*, **34**, 115–127.

Young J (1991) **"Does mummy not want to see me?" Preparing a three-year-old for the death of her mother.** In *Death, Dying and Society* (ed. C Newnes), pp. 386–397. Hove and London: Lawrence Earlbaum Associates.

Yule W & Gold A (1993) *Wise Before the Event. Coping with Crises in Schools*. London: Calouste Gulbenkian Foundation.

Clinical guidelines

None identified.

Reviews

Benjamin S & Eminson D (1992) **Abnormal illness behaviour: childhood experiences and long-term consequences**. *International Review of Psychiatry*, **4**, 55–70.

Fritz G K, Fritsch S & Hagino O (1997) **Somatoform disorders in children and adolescents: a review of the past 10 years**. *Journal of the American Academy of Child and Adolescent Psychiatry*, **36**, 1329–1338.

Garralda E (1995) **The management of functional somatic symptoms in children**. In *Treatment of Functional Somatic Symptoms* (eds R Mayou, C Bass & M Sharpe), pp. 353–370. Oxford: Oxford University Press.

Classic papers

Campo J V & Fritsch S (1994) **Somatization in children and adolescents**. *Journal of the American Academy of Child and Adolescent Psychiatry*, **33**, 1223–1235.

El-khatib H E & Dickey T (1995) **Sertraline for body dysmorphic disorder**. *Journal of the American Academy of Child and Adolescent Psychiatry*, **34**, 1404–1405.

Sanders M R, Shepherd R W, Cleghorn G, *et al* (1994) **The treatment of recurrent abdominal pain in children: a controlled comparison of cognitive–behavioral family intervention and standard pediatric care**. *Journal of Consulting Clinical Psychology*, **62**, 515–529.

Vereker M (1992) **Chronic fatigue syndrome: a joint paediatric-psychiatric approach**. *Archives of Disease in Childhood*, **67**, 550–555.

Cutting edge papers

Albertini R S, Phillips K A & Guevremont (1996) **Body dysmorphic disorder**. *Journal of the American Academy of Child and Adolescent Psychiatry*, **35**, 1425–1426.

Garrald M E (1996) **Somatisation in children**. *Journal of Child Psychiatry and Psychology*, **37**, 13–33.

Systematic reviews and meta-analyses

Myhr G (1998) **Autism and other pervasive developmental disorders: exploring the dimensional view**. *Canadian Journal of Psychiatry*, **43**, 589–595.

Szatmari P (1992) **The validity of autistic spectrum disorders: a literature review**. *Journal of Autism and Developmental Disorders*, **22**, 583–600.

Volkmar F R (1998) **Categorical approaches to the diagnosis of autism: an overview of DSM–IV and ICD–10**. *Autism*, **21**, 45–59.

Clinical guidelines

Kugler B (1998) **The differentiation between autism and Asperger's syndrome**. *Autism*, **2**, 11–32.

Wing L (1997) **The autistic spectrum**. *Lancet*, **350**, 1761–1766.

Classic papers

Asperger H (1991) **Autistic psychopathy in childhood**. In *Autism and Asperger's Syndrome* (trans and annotated by U Frith (ed)), pp. 93–121. New York: Cambridge University Press.

Bishop D (1989) **Autism, Asperger's syndrome and semantic–pragmatic disorder: where are the boundaries?** *British Journal of Disorders of Communication*, **24**,107–121.

Wing L (1981) **Asperger's syndrome: a clinical account**. *Psychological Medicine*, **11**, 115–129.

Wolff S (1991) **'Schizoid' personality in childhood and adult life. I: the vagaries of diagnostic labelling**. *British Journal of Psychiatry*, **159**, 615–620.

——, Townshend R, McGuire R J, *et al* (1991) **'Schizoid' personality in childhood and adult life. II: Adult adjustment and the continuity with schizotypal personality disorder**. *British Journal of Psychiatry*, **159**, 620–629.

Cutting edge papers

Klim A, Volmar F R, Sparrow S S, *et al* (1995) **Validity and neuropsychology characterisation of Asperger's syndrome: convergence with non-verbal learning disability syndrome**. *Journal of Child Psychology and Psychiatry*, **37**, 1127–1140.

Miller J M & Ozanoff S (1997) **Did Asperger's cases have Asperger's disorder? A research note**. *Journal of Child Psychology and Psychiatry*, **38**, 247–251.

Robertson J M (1999) **Domains of social communication handicap in autistic spectrum disorder**. *Journal of American Academy of Child and Adolescent Psychiatry*, **38**, 738–745.

Books

Attwood T (1998) *Asperger's Syndrome – a Guide for Parents and Professionals*. London: Jessica Kingsley.

Happe F (1994) *Autism: an Introduction to Psychological Theory*. London: University College London Press.

Klin A & Volkmar F R (1997) **Asperger's syndrome**. In *Handbook of Autism and Pervasive Developmental Disorders* (eds D J Cohen & F R Volkmar), pp. 94–122. New York: John Wiley and Sons.

Cochrane Controlled Trials Register
9 hits (keywords: pervasive developmental disorder*)
0 hits (keywords: aspergers syndrome)

Cochrane Developmental, Psychosocial and Learning Problems Group
Contact: Ms Jane Dennis, Bristol, UK. e–mail: J.Dennis@bristol.ac.uk

PERVASIVE DEVELOPMENTAL DISORDERS: autism

Systematic reviews and meta-analyses

Yirmiya N, Erel O, Shaked M, *et al* (1998) **Meta-analyses comparing theory of mind abilities of individuals with autism, individuals with mental retardation, and normally developing individuals**. *Psychological Bulletin*, **124**, 283–307.

Clinical guidelines

Freeman B J (1997) **Guidelines for evaluating intervention programs for children with autism**. *Journal of Autism and Developmental Disorders*, **27**, 641–651.

Simonoff E (1998) **Genetic counselling in autism and pervasive developmental disorders**. *Journal of Autism and Developmental Disorders*, **28** (special issue), 447–456.

Reviews

Bailey A, Phillips W & Rutter M (1996) **Autism: towards an integration of clinical, genetic, neuropsychological and neurobiological perspectives**. *Journal of Child Psychology and Psychiatry and Allied Disciplines*, **37**, 89–126.

——, Le Couteur A, Palfreman S, *et al* (1998) **Autism: the phenotype in relatives**. *Journal of Autism and Developmental Disorders*, **28** (special issue), 369–392.

Campbell M, Anderson L T, Small, *et al* (1993) **Naltrexone in autistic children: behavioural symptoms and attentional learning**. *Journal of the American Academy of Child and Adolescent Psychiatry*, **32**, 1283–1291.

Fombonne E (1999) **The epidemiology of autism: a review**. *Psychological Medicine*, **29**, 769–786.

Happe F & Frith U (1996) **The neuropsychology of autism**. *Brain*, **119**, 1377–1400.

Howlin P (1997) **Prognosis in autism: do specialist treatments affect long-term outcome?** *European Child and Adolescent Psychiatry*, **6**, 55–72.

—— (1998) **Practitioner review: psychological and educational treatments for autism**. *Journal of Child Psychology and Psychiatry and Allied Disciplines*, **39**, 307–322.

Pennington B & Ozonoff S (1996) **Executive Functions and Developmental Psychopathology**. *Journal of Child Psychology and Psychiatry*, **37**, 51–87.

Towbin K E (1997) **Autism and Asperger's syndrome**. *Current Opinion in Pediatrics*, **9**, 361–366.

Vostanis P, Smith B, Chung M C, *et al* (1994) **Early detection of childhood autism: a review of screening instructions and rating scales**. *Child: Care, Health and Development*, **20**, 165–177.

Classic papers

Bailey A, Le Couteur A, Gottesman I, *et al* (1995) **Autism as a strongly genetic disorder: evidence from a British twin study**. *Psychological Medicine*, **25**, 63–77.

Bolton P, MacDonald H, Pickles A, *et al* (1994) **A case control family history study of autism**. *Journal of Child Psychology and Psychiatry*, **35**, 887–900.

——, ——, ——, *et al* (1998) **Autism: the point of view from fragile X studies**. *Journal of Autism and Developmental Disorders*, **28** (special issue), 393–406.

Pickles A, Bolton P, MacDonald H, *et al* (1995) **Latent class analysis of recurrence risks for complex phenotypes with selection and measurement error: a twin and family history study of autism**. *American Journal of Human Genetics*, **57**, 717–726.

Rutter M (1996) **Autism research: prospects and priorities**. *Journal of Autism and Developmental Disorders*, **26**, 257–275.

Smalley S (1998) **Autism and tuberous sclerosis**. *Journal of Autism and Developmental Disorders*, **28** (special issue), 407–414.

Cutting edge papers

Bailey A, Luthert P, Harding B, *et al* (1998) **A clinicopathological study of autism**. *Brain*, **121**, 889–905.

International Molecular Genetics Study of Autism Consortium (1998) **A full genome screen for autism with evidence for linkage to a region on chromosome 7q**. *Human Molecular Genetics*, **7**, 571–578.

McDougle C, Naylor S T, Cohen, D J, *et al* (1996) **A double-blind, placebo-controlled study of fluvoxamine in adults with autistic disorder**. *Archives of General Psychiatry*, 53, 1001–1008.

Nicoll A, Elliman D & Ross E (1998) **MMR vaccination and autism 1998**. *British Medical Journal*, **316**, 715–716.

Piven J, Arndt S, Bailey J, *et al* (1996) **Regional brain enlargement in autism: a magnetic imaging study**. *Journal of the American Academy of Adolescent Psychiatry*, **35**, 530–536.

Woodhouse W, Bailey A, Bolton P, *et al* (1996) **Head circumference and pervasive developmental disorder**. *Journal of Child Psychology and Psychiatry*, **37**, 665–671.

Reports

Best L & Miln R (1997) *Auditory Integration Training in Autism*. Southampton: Wessex Institute for Health Research and Development.

Books

Howlin P (1998) *Children with Autism and Asperger's Syndrome: a Guide for Practitioners and Carers*. Chichester: John Wiley and Sons.

Rutter M, Bailey A, Simonoff E, *et al* (1997) **Genetic influences and autism**. In *A Handbook of Autism and Pervasive Developmental Disorders* (eds D J Cohen & F R Volkmar), pp. 370–387. New York: John Wiley and Sons.

Volkmar F R (1998) *Autism and Pervasive Developmental Disorders*.
Cambridge: Cambridge University Press.

Cochrane Controlled Trials Register
9 hits (keywords: pervasive developmental disorder*)
0 hits (keywords: aspergers syndrome)

Cochrane Developmental, Psychosocial and Learning Problems Group
Contact: Ms Jane Dennis, Bristol, UK. e-mail: J.Dennis@bristol.ac.uk

POST-TRAUMATIC STRESS DISORDER

Systematic reviews and meta-analyses

Stein D J, Zungu-Dirwayi N & Van der Linden G (1998) **Pharmacotherapy for post traumatic stress disorder**. Protocol for a Cochrane Review. In *The Cochrane Library*. Issue 1. Oxford: Update Software.

Wessely S, Rose S & Bisson J (1997) **Brief psychological interventions ("debriefing") for treating trauma-related symptoms and preventing post traumatic stress disorder**. Cochrane Review. In *The Cochrane Library*, Issue 1. Oxford: Update Software.

Clinical guidelines

American Academy of Child and Adolescent Psychiatry (1998) **Practice parameters for the assessment and treatment of children and adolescents with post-traumatic stress disorder**. *Journal of the American Academy of Child and Adolescent Psychiatry*, **37** (suppl.), S4–S26.

American Psychiatric Association (1994) *Diagnostic and Statistical Manual of Mental Disorders* (4th edn)(DSM–IV). Washington, DC: American Psychiatric Association.

World Health Organization (1992) *The International Classification of Diseases and Related Disorders* (ICD–10). Geneva: World Health Organization.

Reviews

Pfefferbaum B (1998) **Post-Traumatic Stress Disorder in Children: a review of the past 10 years**. *Journal of the American Academy of Child and Adolescent Psychiatry*, **36**, 1503–1511.

Udwin O (1993) **Children's reactions to traumatic events**. *Journal of Child Psychology and Psychiatry*, **34**, 115–127.

Yule W (1994) **Post traumatic stress disorder**. In *Child and Adolescent Psychiatry: Modern Approaches* (eds M Rutter, E Taylor & L Hersov), pp. 392–406. Oxford: Blackwell Scientific Publications.

Classic papers

Busuttil A M C & Busuttil W (1995) **Psychological debriefing**. *British Journal of Psychiatry*, **166**, 676–677.

Horowitz M, Wilner N & Alvariz W (1979) **Impact of event scale: a measure of subjective stress**. *Psychosomatic Medicine*, **41**, 209–218.

Lansdown R & Benjamin G (1985) **The development of the concept of death in children aged 5–9 years**. *Child: Care, Health and Development*, **11**, 13–20.

Pynoos R S (1987) **Life threat and post traumatic stress in school-age children**. *Archives of General Psychiatry*, **44**, 1057–1063.

Speece M W & Brent S B (1984) **Children's understanding of death: a review of three components of a death concept**. *Child Development*, **55**, 1671–1686.

Terr L C (1983) **Chowcilla revisited: the effects of psychic trauma four years after schoolbus kidnapping**. *American Journal of Psychiatry*, **140**, 1543–1550.

Cutting edge papers

Biederman J, Klein R, Pine D, *et al* (1998) **Resolved: mania is mistaken for ADHD in prepubertal children**. *Journal of the American Academy of Child and Adolescent Psychiatry*, **37**, 1091–1099.

Costello E J, Angold A, March J, *et al* (1998) **Life events and post traumatic stress: the development of a new measure for children and adolescents.** *Psychological Medicine*, **28**, 1275–1288.

Scheeringa M S, Zeanah C H, Drell M J, *et al* (1995) **Two approaches to the diagnosis of post-traumatic stress disorder in infancy and early childhood**. *Journal of the American Academy of Child and Adolescent Psychiatry*, **34**, 191–200.

Shapiro F (1989) **Eye movement desensitization: a new treatment for post-traumatic stress disorder**. *Journal of Behavioural Therapy and Experimental Psychiatry*, **20**, 211–217.

Summerfield D (1998) Chapter 1. In *Rethinking the Trauma of War* (eds P Bracken & C Petty). London & New York: Free Association Books Ltd.

Books

Black D, Harris-Hendriks J & Kaplan T (1993) *When Father Kills Mother: Guiding Children Through Trauma and Grief*. London: Routledge.

——, Newman M, Harris-Hendriks J, *et al* (1997) *Psychological Trauma: a Developmental Approach*. London: Gaskell.

Further reading

Black D, Harris–Hendricks J & Kaplan T (1993) *When Fathers Kills Mother: Guiding Children through Trauma and Grief*. London: Routledge.

——, Newman M, Harris–Hendricks J, *et al* (1997) *Psychological Trauma: a Developmental Approach*. London: Gaskell.

Mayou R, Bryant B & Duthie R (1993) **Psychiatric consequences of road traffic accidents**. *British Medical Journal*, **307**, 647–651.

Stallard P & Law F (1993) **Screening and psychological debriefing of adolescent survivors of life-threatening events**. *British Journal of Psychiatry*, **163**, 660–665.

Cochrane Controlled Trials Register
4 hits (keywords: post traumatic stress AND child*)
2 hits (keywords: post traumatic stress AND adolescen*)

Cochrane Depression, Anxiety and Neurosis Group
Contact: Review Group Coordinator: Miss Natalie Khin, New Zealand;
e-mail: n.khin@auckland.ac.nz

PSYCHOSIS: mania and bipolar affective disorder

Systematic reviews and meta-analyses

Geller B & Luby J (1997) **Child and adolescent bipolar disorder: a review of the past 10 years**. *Journal of the American Academy of Child and Adolescent Psychiatry*, **36**, 1168–1176.

Lapalme M, Hodgins S & LaRoche C (1997) **Children of parents with bipolar disorder: a meta-analysis of risk for mental disorders**. *Canadian Journal of Psychiatry*, **42**, 623–631.

Weller E B, Weller R A & Fristad M A (1995) **Bipolar disorder in children: misdiagnosis underdiagnosis, and future directions**. *Journal of the American Academy of Child and Adolescent Psychiatry*, **34**, 709–714.

Clinical guidelines

American Academy of Child and Adolescent Psychiatry (1997) **Practice parameters for the assessment and treatment of children and adolescents with bipolar disorders**. *Journal of the American Academy of Child and Adolescent Psychiatry*, **36** (suppl.), 157S–173S.

Reviews

Botteron K N & Geller B (1995) **Pharmacological treatment of childhood and adolescent mania**. *Child and Adolescent Psychiatric Clinics of North America*, **4**, 283–304.

Geller B & Luby J (1997) **Child and adolescent bipolar disorder: a review of the past 10 years**. *Journal of the American Academy of Child and Adolescent Psychiatry*, **36**, 1168–1176.

Classic papers

Anthony E J & Scott P (1960) **Manic depressive psychosis in childhood**. *Journal of Child Psychology and Psychiatry*, **1**, 53–72.

Kraepelin E (1921) *Manic Depressive Insanity and Paranore*. Edinburgh: Livingstone.

Loranger A P W & Levine P M (1978) **Age of onset of bipolar affective illness**. *Archives of General Psychiatry*, **35**, 1345–1348.

Cutting edge papers

Geller B, Cooper T B, Sun K, *et al* (1998) **Double-blind placebo-controlled study of lithium for adolescents with comorbid bipolar and substance dependency**. *Journal of the American Academy of Child and Adolescent Psychiatry*, **37**, 171–178.

Remschmidt H (1998) **Bipolar disorders in children and adolescents**. *Current Opinion in Psychiatry*, **11**, 379–383.

Sigurdsson E, Fombonne E, Sayal K, *et al* (1999) **Neurodevelopmental antecedents of early-onset bipolar affective disorder**. *British Journal of Psychiatry*, **174**, 121–127.

Woolston J L (1999) **Case study: carbamazepine treatment of juvenile-onset bipolar disorder**. *Journal of the American Academy of Child and Adolescent Psychiatry*, **38**, 335–338.

PSYCHOSIS: schizophrenia

Systematic reviews and meta-analyses

Hollis C & Taylor E (1997) **Schizophrenia: a critique from the developmental psychopathology perspective**. In *Neurodevelopment and Adult Psychopathology* (eds M S Keshervan & R M Murray). Cambridge: Cambridge University Press.

Jacobson L & Rapoport J (1998) **Research update: childhood–onset schizophrenia: implications for clinical and neurobiological research**. *Journal of Child Psychology and Psychiatry*, **39**, 101–113.

Joy C B, Adams C E & Lawrie S M (1998) **Haloperidol for schizophrenia.** Protocol for a Cochrane Review. In *The Cochrane Library*. Issue 1. Oxford: Update Software.

Nicol M M, Robertson L & Connaughton J A (1998) **Life skills programmes for people with chronic mental illness**. Cochrane Review. In *The Cochrane Library*. Issue 1. Oxford: Update Software.

Rey J M & Walter G (1997) **Half a century of ECT use in young people**. *American Journal of Psychiatry*, **54**, 500–602.

Srisurapanont M, Disayavanish C & Taimkaew K (1999) **Quetiapine for schizophrenia**. Cochrane Review. In *The Cochrane Library*. Issue 1. Oxford: Update Software.

Tuunainen A & Gilbody S M (2000) **Newer atypical antipsychotic medication versus clopapine for schizophrenia**. Cochrane Review. In *The Cochrane Library*. Issue 1. Oxford: Update Software.

Clinical guidelines

American Academy of Child and Adolescent Psychiatry (1994) **Practice parameters for the assessment and treatment of children and adolescents with schizophrenia**. *Journal of American Academy of Child and Adolescent Psychiatry*, **33**, 616–635.

Clark A & Lewis S (1998) **Treatment of schizophrenia in childhood and adolescence**. *Journal of Child Psychology and Psychiatry*, **39**, 1071–1081.

Hollis C P (2000) **Adolescent schizophrenia**. *Advances in Psychiatric Treatment*, **6**, 83–92.

McCellan J M & Werry J S (1994) **Practice parameters for the assessment and treatment of children and adolescents with schizophrenia**. *Journal of the American Academy of Child and Adolescent Psychiatry*, **33**, 616–635.

Reviews

Werry J S & Taylor E (1994) **Schizophrenia and allied disorders**. In *Child and Adolescent Psychiatry: Modern Approaches* (eds M Rutter & E Taylor), pp. 594–615. Oxford: Blackwell Scientific.

Classic papers

Kallman F J & Roth B (1956) **Genetic aspects of preadolescent schizophrenia**. *American Journal of Psychiatry*, **112**, 599–606.

Kolvin I (1971) **Studies in the childhood psychoses: I. Diagnostic criteria and classification**. *British Journal of Psychiatry*, **118**, 381–384.

Rutter M (1972) **Childhood schizophrenia reconsidered**. *Journal of Autism and Childhood Schizophrenia*, **2**, 315–407.

$(\text{Cutting edge papers})$

Alaghband–Rad J, Hamburger S D, Giedd J, *et al* (1997) **Childhood-onset schizophrenia: biological markers in relation to clinical characteristics**. *American Journal of Psychiatry*, **154**, 64–68.

Frazier J A, Geidd J N, Kaysen D, *et al* (1996) **Childhood-onset schizophrenia: brain magnetic imaging rescan after two years of clozapine maintenance**. *American Journal of Psychiatry*, **153**, 564–566.

Kuma S, Frazier J A, Jacobson L K, *et al* (1996) **Childhood-onset schizophrenia: a double-blind clozapine–haloperidol comparison**. *Archives of General Psychiatry*, **53**, 1090–1097.

Cochrane Controlled Trials Register
12 hits (keywords: psychosis AND child*)
51 hits (keywords: psychosis AND adolescen*)
67 hits (keywords: schizophrenia AND child*)
375 hits (keywords: schizophrenia AND adolescen*)

Cochrane Depression, Anxiety and Neurosis Group
Contact: Review Group Coordinator: Miss Natalie Khin, New Zealand;
e-mail: n.khin@auckland.ac.nz

SUBSTANCE MISUSE

Systematic reviews and meta-analyses

Bangert-Drowns R L (1988) **The effects of school-based substance abuse education – a meta-analysis.** *Journal of Drug Education*, **18**, 243–264.

Ennett S T, Tobler N S, Ringwalt C L, *et al* (1994) **How effective is drug abuse resistance education? A meta-analysis of Project DARE outcome evaluations.** *American Journal of Public Health*, **84**, 394–1401.

Fillmore K M, Hartka E, Johnstone B M, *et al* (1991) **The Collaborative Alcohol-Related Longitudinal Project. A meta-analysis of life course variation in drinking.** *British Journal of Addiction to Alcohol and Other Drugs*, **86**, 1221–1268.

——, ——, ——, *et al* (1991) **The Collaborative Alcohol-Related Longitudinal Project. Preliminary results from a meta-analysis of drinking behaviour in multiple longitudinal studies.** *British Journal of Addiction to Alcohol and Other Drugs*, **86**, 1221–1268.

Foxcroft D R & Lowe G (1991) **Adolescent drinking behaviour and family socialization factors: a meta-analysis.** *Journal of Adolescence*, **14**, 255–273.

——, Lister-Sharp D & Lowe G (1997) **Alcohol misuse prevention for young people: a systematic review reveals methodological concerns and lack of reliable evidence of effectiveness.** *Addiction*, **92**, 531–537.

Gowing L, Ali R & White J (1999) **Opioid dependence: combined use of opioid antagonists and adrenergic agonists to induce withdrawal from heroin and other short acting opiates without sedation or anaesthesia.** Protocol for a Cochrane Review. In *The Cochrane Library*. Issue 1. Oxford: Update Software.

Johnstone B M, Leino E V, Ager C R, *et al* (1996) **Determinants of life-course variation in the frequency of alcohol consumption: meta-analysis of studies from the collaborative alcohol-related longitudinal project.** *Journal of Studies on Alcohol*, **57**, 494–506.

Kirchmayer U, Davoli M & Verster A (1999) **Naltrexone maintenance treatment for opioid dependence.** Protocol for a Cochrane Review. In *The Cochrane Library*. Issue 1. Oxford: Update Software.

Lima A R, Lima M S, Churchill R, *et al* (1999) **Carbamazepine for cocaine dependence.** Protocol for a Cochrane Review. In *The Cochrane Library*. Issue 1. Oxford: Update Software.

Minozzi S & Grilli R (1997) **The systematic review of studies on the efficacy of interventions for the primary prevention of alcohol abuse among adolescents.** *Epidemiologia e Prevenzione*, **21**, 180–188.

Stead M & Hastings G (1995) **Developing options for a programme on adolescent smoking in Wales.** *Health Promotion Wales Technical Report*, **16**, 32.

Tobler N S (1997) **Effectiveness of school-based drug prevention programs: a meta-analysis of the research.** *Journal of Primary Prevention*, **18**, 71–128.

Clinical guidelines

American Academy of Child and Adolescent Psychiatry (1998) **Practice parameters for the assessment and treatment of children and adolescents with substance use disorders**. *Journal of the American Academy of Child and Adolescent Psychiatry*, **36** (suppl.) 140S–156S.

American Psychiatric Association (1995) **Practice guideline for treatment of patients with substance use disorders: alcohol, cocaine, opioids**. *American Journal of Psychiatry*, **152** (suppl.), 1–59.

Najavits L M & Weiss R D (1994) **Variations in therapist effectiveness in the treatment of patients with substance use disorders: an empirical review**. *Addiction*, **89**, 679–688.

USA Substance Abuse and Mental Health Services Administration (1999) *Screening and Assessing Adolescents for Substance Use Disorders*. www.nlm.nih.gov/libserv.html

Cutting edge papers

Geller B (1998) **Double-blind placebo-controlled study of lithium for adolescents with bipolar disorders with secondary substance dependency**. *Journal of the American Academy of Child and Adolescent Psychiatry*, *37*, 171–178.

Reports

Ghelani P (1998) *Volatile Substance Abuse*. Report 160. London: National Children's Bureau.

Jarvis L (1996) *Smoking Among Secondary School Children in 1996 in England*. London: The Stationary Office.

—— (1996) *Teenage Smoking Attitudes in 1996: a Survey of the Smoking Behaviour, Knowledge and Attitudes of 11- to 15-Year-Olds in England*. London: The Stationary Office.

Mounteney J (1998) *Children of Drug-Using Parents*. Report 163. London: National Children's Bureau.

SCODA & The Children's Legal Centre (1999) *Policy Guidance for Drug Intervention*. London: SCODA.

Cochrane Controlled Trials Register
2 hits (keywords: substance misuse)
113 hits (keywords: drug abuse" AND adolescen*)
64 hits (keywords: cocaine AND adolescen*)
54 hits (keywords: marijuana AND abuse)
24 hits (keywords: cannabis AND abuse)
95 hits (keywords: opiate* AND abuse)

Systematic reviews and meta-analyses

Durlak J A, Fuhrman T & Lampman C (1991) **Effectiveness of cognitive–behavioural therapy for maladaptive children: a meta-analysis.** *Psychological Bulletin*, **110**, 204–214.

Dush D M, Hirt M L & Schroeder H E (1989) **Self-statement modification in the treatment of child behaviour disorders: a meta-analysis.** *Psychological Bulletin*, **106**, 97–106.

Harrington R, Whittaker J, Shoebridge P, *et al* (1998) **Systematic review of efficacy of cognitive–behavioural therapies in childhood and adolescent depressive disorder.** *British Medical Journal*, **316**, 1559–1563.

Reinecke M A, Ryan N E & Dubois D L (1998) **Cognitive–behavioural therapy of depression and depressive symptoms during adolescence: a review and meta-analysis.** *Journal of the American Academy of Child and Adolescent Psychiatry*, **37**, 26–34.

Reviews

Harrington R, Whittaker J & Shoebridge P (1998) **Psychological treatment of depression in children and adolescents: a review of treatment research.** *British Journal of Psychiatry*, **173**, 291–298.

Indoe D (1995) **Cognitive–behavioural therapy and children of the code.** *Educational and Child Psychology*, **12**, 71–81.

Target M & Fonagy P (1996) **The psychological treatment of child and adolescent psychiatric disorders.** In *What Works for Whom?* (eds A Roth & P Fonagy). London: Guildford Press.

Cutting edge papers

Brent D, Holder D, Kolko D, *et al* (1997) **A clinical psychotherapy trial for adolescent depression comparing cognitive, family and supportive treatments.** *Archives of General Psychiatry*, **54**, 877–885.

Kendell P C (1994) **Treating anxiety disorders in children: results of a randomized clinical trial.** *Journal of Consulting and Clinical Psychology*, **62**, 100–110.

Treasure J L, Katzman M, Schmidt U, *et al* (1999) **Engagement and outcome in the treatment of bulimia nervosa: first phase of a sequential design comparing motivational enhancement therapy and cognitive–behavioural therapy.** *Behaviour Research and Therapy*, **37**, 405–418.

Wood A J, Harrington R C & Moore A (1996) **Controlled trial of a brief cognitive–behavioural intervention in adolescent patients with depression.** *Journal of Child Psychology and Psychiatry*, **37**, 727–746.

Reports

Best L & Stevens A (1996) *Cognitive–Behavioural Therapy in the Treatment of Chronic Fatigue Syndrome*. Report 50. Development and Evaluation Committee.

Royal College of Psychiatrists (1997) *Guidelines to Good Practice in the Use of Behavioural and Cognitive Treatments: Report of a Working Party of the Royal College of Psychiatrists*. London: Royal College of Psychiatrists.

Books

Braswell L & Bloomquist M (1991) *Cognitive Behavioural Therapy with ADHD Children: Child, Family and School Interventions*. New York: Guildford Press.

Graham P (ed.) (1998) *Cognitive–Behavioural Therapy for Children and Families*. Cambridge: Cambridge University Press.

Kendall P C (ed.) (1991) *Child and Adolescent Therapy: Cognitive Behavioural Procedures*. New York: Guildford Press.

Meyers A M & Craighead W E (eds) (1984) *Cognitive Behaviour Therapy with Children*. New York: Plenum Press.

THERAPEUTIC APPROACHES: family therapy

Systematic reviews and meta-analyses

Heekerens H P (1991) **Evaluation of family therapy. What is the value of a new treatment approach in paediatric and adolescent problems?** *Acta Paedopschiatrica*, **54**, 56–67.

Mari J J & Streiner D (1996) **Family intervention reduces relapse rates, rehospitalisation, and costs and increases compliance with medication in schizophrenia.** Cochrane Review. In *The Cochrane Library*. Issue 1. Oxford: Update Software.

Markus E, Lange A & Petigrew T F (1990) **Effectiveness of family therapy: a meta-analysis.** *Journal of Family Therapy*, **12**, 205–221.

Panton J & White E A (1999) **Family therapy for asthma in children.** Cochrane Review. In *The Cochrane Library*. Issue 4. Oxford: Update Software.

Shadish W R, Ragsdaly K, Glaser R R, *et al* (1995) **The efficacy and effectiveness of marital and family therapy: a perspective from meta-analysis.** *Journal of Marital and Family Therapy*, **21**, 345–360.

Reviews

Carr A (1991) **Milan systemic family therapy: a review of ten empirical investigations.** *Journal of Family Therapy*, **13**, 237–263.

Chamberlain P & Rosicky J G (1995) **The effectiveness of family therapy in the treatment of adolescents with conduct disorders and delinquency.** *Journal of Marital and Family Therapy*, **21**, 441–459.

Estrada A U & Pinsof W M (1995) **The effectiveness of family therapies for selected behavioural disorders of childhood.** *Journal of Marital and Family Therapy*, **21**, 403–440.

Heekerens H P (1991) **Evaluation of family therapy. What is the value of a new treatment approach in paediatric and adolescent problems?** *Acta Paedopsychiatrica*, **54**, 56–67.

Pinsof W & Wynne L (1995) **The efficacy of marital and family therapy: an empirical overview, conclusions and recommendations.** *Journal of Marital and Family Therapy*, **21**, 585–613.

Waldron H B (1997) **Adolescent substance abuse and family therapy outcome. A review of randomised trials.** *Advances in Clinical Psychology*, **19**, 199–234.

Classic papers

Andersen T (1987) **The reflecting-team: dialogue and meta-dialogue in clinical work.** *Family Process*, **26**, 415–428.

Selvini Palazolli M, Boscolo L, Cecchin G, *et al* (1980) **Hypothesizing–circularity–neurality: three guidelines for the conductor of the session.** *Family Process*, **19**, 3–12.

Cutting edge papers

Beavers R W & Hampson R B (1996) **Measuring family therapy outcome in a clinical setting: families that do better or do worse in therapy**. *Family Process*, **35**, 347–361.

Campbell D (1999) **Family therapy and beyond: where is the Milan systemic approach today?** *Child Psychology and Psychiatry Review*, **4**, 76–84.

Huffington C (1999) **Containing failure: consultancy to a residential centre for adolescents**. *Clinical Child Psychiatry and Psychology*, **4**, 533–541.

White M (1984) **Pseudo-encopresis: from avalanche to victory, from vicious to virtuous cycles**. *Family Systems Medicine*, **2**, 150–160.

Practice considerations

Goldberg D & Hodges M (1992) **The poison of racism and the self-poisoning of adolescents**. *Journal of Family Therapy*, **14**, 51–68.

Kingston P & Smith D (1983) **Preparation for live consultation and live supervision when working without a one-way screen**. *Journal of Family Therapy*, **5**, 219–233.

Reder P (1986) **Multi-agency family systems**. *Journal of Family Therapy*, **8**, 139–152.

Tuffnell G (1993) **Judgements of Solomon: the relevance of a systems approach to psychiatric court reports in child care cases**. *Journal of Family Therapy*, **15**, 413–432.

Usher J M (1991) **Family and couples therapy with gay and lesbian clients: acknowledging the forgotten minority**. *Journal of Family Therapy*, **13**, 131–148.

Books

Burnham J (1986) *Family Therapy*. London: Tavistock Publications.

Byng–Hall J (1995) *Rewriting Family Scripts*. New York: Guildford Press.

Gorell Barnes G (1998) *Family Therapy in Changing Times*. London: MacMillan Press.

THERAPEUTIC APPROACHES: group treatments

Systematic reviews and meta-analyses

Dalal F (1997) **A transcultural perspective on psychodynamic psychotherapy addressing internal and external realities**. *Group Analysis*, **30**, 203–215.

Hoag M J & Burlingame G M (1997) **Evaluating effectiveness of child and adolescent group treatment: a meta-analytic review**. *Journal of Clinical Child Psychology*, **26**, 234–246. Reviewed on DARE.

Hyde K (1988) **Analytic group psychotherapies**. In **Group Therapy in Britain** (eds M Areline & W Dryden), pp. 13–42. Open University Press.

Clinical guidelines

Brown R, Domingo-Perez L & Murphy D (1989) **Treating 'impossible' children: a therapeutic group on a children's ward**. *Group Analysis*, **22**, 283–298.

Del Balzo V & Judges T (1998) **Toward socialisation: the seriously disturbed adolescent in group psychotherapy**. *Group Analysis*, **31**, 157–171.

Woods J (ed.) (1996) **Group analysis with children, families and young people**. *Group Analysis*, **29**, 5–98.

Reviews

Dishion T J, McCord J & Toulin F (1999) **When interventions harm: peer group and problem behaviour**. *American Psychologist*, **54**, 755–764.

Classic papers

Cox M (1973) **Group Psychotherapy as a redefining process**. *International Journal of Group Psychotherapy*, **23**, 465–473.

Harrison T & Clarke D (1992) **The Northfield Experiments**. *British Journal of Psychiatry*, **160**, 698–708.

Pines M (ed.) (1983) **The contribution of S H Foulkes to group therapy**. In **The Evolution of Group Analysis.** Pp. 265–285. London: Routledge & Keegan Page.

Cutting edge papers

Davidson B (1999) **Writing as a tool of reflective practice. Sketches and reflections from inside the split milieu of an eating disorders unit**. *Group Analysis*, **32**, 109–124.

Nitsun M (1991) **The anti-group: destructive forces in the group and their therapeutic potential**. *Group Analysis*, **24**, 7–20.

Wood D (1999) **From silent scream to shared sadness**. *Group Analysis*, **32**, 53–70.

Books

Kennard D, Roberts J & Winter D A (1993) *A Work Book of Group Analytic Interventions*. London: Routledge.

Dwivedi K N (1993) *Groupwork with Children and Adolescents*. London: Jessica Kingsley.

THERAPEUTIC APPROACHES: music therapy

Papers

Brown S (1994) **Autism and music therapy: is change possible, and why music?** *British Journal of Music Therapy*, **8**, 15–25.

Dun B (1995) **A different beat: music therapy in children's cardiac care.** *Music Therapy Perspectives*, **13**, 35–39.

Friedlander L H (1994) **Group music psychotherapy in an in-patient psychiatric setting for children: a developmental approach.** *Music Therapy Perspectives*, **12,** 92–97.

Goodman K D (1989) **Music therapy assessment of emotionally disturbed children.** *Arts in Psychotherapy*, **16**, 179–192.

Montello L & Coons E E (1998) **Effects of active versus passive group music therapy on preadolescents with emotional, learning and behavioural disorders.** *Journal of Music Therapy*, **35**, 49–67.

Rogers P (1995) **Childhood sexual abuse: dilemmas in therapeutic practice.** *Music Therapy Perspectives*, **13**, 24–30.

Schogler B (1998) **Music as a tool in communications research.** *Nordic Journal of Music Therapy*, **7**, 40–49.

Smeijsters H (1996) **Music therapy with anorexia nervosa: an integrative theoretical and methodological perspective.** *British Journal of Music Therapy*, **10**. 3–13.

Books

Aldridge D (1996) *Music Therapy Research and Practice in Medicine: from Out of the Silence*. London: Jessica Kingsley.

Wigram T & De Backer J (eds) (1999) *Clinical Applications of Music Therapy in Developmental Disability, Paediatrics and Neurology*. London: Jessica Kingsley.

Specialist library

The **Nordoff–Robbins Music Therapy Centre**, 2 Lissenden Gardens, London NW5 1PP. Tel: 020 7267 4496 (a private reference library, visits by appointment only).

General information on music therapy

Purchase of books and journals: most current publications, including the *British Journal of Music Therapy*, can be ordered from the British Society for Music Therapy, 25 Rosslyn Avenue, East Barnet, Hertfordshire EH4 8DT. Tel: 020 8368 8879; e-mail: denize@bsmt.demon.co.uk

Internet and other electronic resources

http://www.roehampton.ac.uk/academic/artsandhum/bsmst/bsmt.html
http://www.musictherapy.org/index.html

http://www.hisf.no/njmt http://www.nordoff-robbins.org.uk

Databases include:

CAIRSS (Computer-Assisted Information Retrieval Service System (net address: http://sherlock.utsa.edu/)

Music Therapy INFO (not internet connected), Vols 1 and 2 CD-ROMS (freeware) from Professor David Aldridge, Institute for Music Therapy, Faculty of Medicine, University of Witten-Herdecke, Alfred-Herrhausen Str. 50, D-58448, Witten, Germany; e-mail: davida@uni-sh.de RILM (Répertoire Internationale de Littérature Musicale) database/CD-ROM – www.aub.auc.dk

Systematic reviews and meta-analyses

Hartmann A, Herzog T & Drinkman A (1992) **Psychotherapy of bulimia nervosa: what is effective? A meta-analysis.** *Journal of Psychosomatic Research*, **2**, 159–167.

Heekerens H P (1989) **Effectiveness of child and adolescent psychotherapy within the scope of meta-analysis.** *Zeitschrift fur Kinder und Jugendpsychiatrie*, **17**, 150–157.

Russell R L, Greenwald S & Shirk S R (1991) **Language change in child psychotherapy: a meta-analytic review.** *Journal of Consulting and Clinical Psychology,* **59**, 916–919.

Weiss B & Weisz J R (1990) **The impact of methodological factors on child psychotherapy outcome research: a meta-analysis for researchers.** *Journal of Consulting and Clinical Psychology*, **54**, 789–795.

Weisz J R, Weiss B, Alicke M D, *et al* (1987) **Effectiveness of psychotherapy with children and adolescents: a meta-analysis for clinicians.** *Journal of Consulting and Clinical Psychology*, **55**, 542–549.

——, Weiss B, Han S S, *et al* (1995) **Effects of psychotherapy with children and adolescents revisited: a meta-analysis of treatment outcome studies.** *Psychological Bulletin*, **117**, 450–468.

——, ——, Morton T, *et al* (1992) **Meta-analysis of psychotherapy outcome research with children and adolescents.** Los Angeles, CA: University of California.

Reviews

Barnett R J, Docherty J P & Frommelt G M (1991) **A review of psychotherapy research since 1963.** *Journal of the American Academy of Child and Adolescent Psychiatry*, **30,** 1–14.

March J S (1995) **Cognitive–behavioural psychotherapy for children and adolescents with OCD: a review and recommendations for treatment.** *Journal of the American Academy of Child and Adolescent Psychiatry*, **34**, 7–18.

Mitchell J E (1991) **A review of the controlled trials of psychotherapy for bulimia nervosa.** *Journal of Psychosomatic Research*, **35**, 23–31.

Najavits L M & Weiss R D (1994) **Variations in therapist effectiveness in the treatment of patients with substance use disorders: an empirical review.** *Addiction*, **89**, 679–688.

Pearsall D F (1997) **Psychotherapy outcome research in child psychiatric disorders.** *Canadian Journal of Psychiatry*, **42**, 595–601.

Weiss B, Catron T, Harris V, *et al* (1994) **The effectiveness of traditional child psychotherapy.** *Journal of Consulting and Clinical Psychology*, **67**, 82–94.

Reports

Russell R L, Greenwald S & Shirk S R (1991) **Language change in child psychotherapy: a meta-analytic review.** *Journal of Consulting and Clinical Psychology*, **59**, 916–919.

TIC DISORDERS: tics and Gilles de la Tourette syndrome

Systematic reviews and meta-analyses

None identified.

Clinical guidelines

None identified.

Reviews

Leckman J F, Peterson B S, Anderson G M, *et al* (1997) **Pathogenesis of Tourette's syndrome**. *Journal of Child Psychology and Psychiatry*, **38**, 119–142.

Robertson M M (1994) **Annotation: Gilles de la Tourette syndrome – an update**. *Journal of Child Psychology and Psychiatry*, **35**, 597–611.

Classic papers

Bliss J (1980) **Sensory experiences of Gilles de la Tourette syndrome**. *Archives of General Psychiatry*, **37**, 1343–1347.

Bruun R D, Shapiro A K, Shapiro E, *et al* (1976) **A follow–up of 78 patients with Gilles de la Tourette syndrome**. *American Journal of Psychiatry*, **133**, 944–947.

Sacks O (1985) *Witty Ticcy Ray. The Man Who Mistook His Wife for a Hat*. London: Duckworth.

Cutting edge papers

Eapen V, Robertson M M, Alsobrook II J P, *et al* (1997) **Obsessive–compulsive disorder in Gilles de la Tourette syndrome and obsessive–compulsive disorder: differences by diagnosis and family history**. *American Journal of Medical Genetics (Neuropsychiatric Genetics)*, **74**, 432–438.

Swedo S E, Leonard H L, Garvey M, *et al* (1998) **Pediatric auto-immune neuropsychiatric disorders associated with streptococcal infections: clinical description of the first 50 cases**. *American Journal of Psychiatry*, **155**, 264–271.

Books

Robertson M M & Baron-Cohen S (1998) *Tourette syndrome: the Facts*. Oxford: Oxford University Press.

Further reading

Apter A, Pauls D L, Bleich A, *et al* (1993) **An epidemiological study of Gilles de la Tourette syndrome in Israel**. *Archives of General Psychiatry*, **9**, 734–738.

Cohen D J (1991) **Tourette's syndrome: a model disorder for integrating psychoanalysis and biological perspectives**. *International Review of Psychoanalysis*, **18**, 195–209.

Leckman J F, Dolnasky E S & Hardin M T (1990) **Perinatal factors in the expression of Tourette's syndrome: an exploratory study.** *Journal of the American Academy of Child and Adolescent Psychiatry,* **29**, 220–206.

Pauls D L, Pakstis A J & Kurlan R (1990) **Segregation and linkage analysis of Gilles de la Tourette syndrome and related disorders.** *Journal of the American Academy of Child and Adolescent Psychiatry,* **29**, 195–203.

Robertson M M & Reinstein D Z (1991) **Convulsive tic disorder. Georges Gilles de la Tourette, Guinon and Grasset on the phenomenology and psychopathology of the Gilles de la Tourette Syndrome.** *Behavioural Neurology,* **4**, 29–56.

Cochrane Controlled Trials Register
0 hits (keywords: tourette's syndrome*)
25 hits (keywords: tics AND child*)

Cochrane Movement Disorders Group
Contact: Review Group Coordinator, Dr Joaquim Ferreire Lisbon, Portugal.
Tel: 351 1797 3453; e-mail: movementdisord@mail.telepac.pt

Section 3: Emerging datasets

Assessment

Clinical guidelines

American Academy of Child and Adolescent Psychiatry (1994) **Practice parameters for the assessment and treatment of children and adolescents with schizophrenia**. *Journal of the American Academy of Child and Adolescent Psychiatry*, **33**, 616–635.

—— (1997) **Practice parameters for the assessment and treatment of children, adolescents and adults with attention–deficit hyperactivity disorder.** *Journal of American Academy of Child Adolescent Psychiatry*, **36** (suppl.), 85S–121S.

—— (1997) **Practice parameters for the assessment and treatment of children and adolescents with conduct disorder**. *Journal of the American Academy of Child and Adolescent Psychiatry*, **36** (suppl.), 122S–139S.

—— (1997) **Practice parameters for the assessment and treatment of children and adolescents with bipolar disorder**. *Journal of the American Academy of Child and Adolescent Psychiatry*, **36**, 138–157.

—— (1997) **Practice parameters for the forensic evaluation of children and adolescents who may have been physically or sexually abused**. *Journal of the American Academy of Child and Adolescent Psychiatry*, **36**, 423–442.

—— (1998) Practice parameters for the psychiatric assessment of children and toddlers. *Abstracts of Clinical Care Guidelines*, **10**, 1–7.

—— (1998) **Practice parameters for the assessment and treatment of children and adolescents with post-traumatic stress disorder**. *Journal of the American Academy of Child and Adolescent Psychiatry*, **37** (suppl.), 4S–26S.

—— (1998) **Practice parameters for the assessment and treatment of children and adolescents with obsessive–compulsive disorder**. *Journal of the American Academy of Child and Adolescent Psychiatry*, **37**(suppl.), 27S–45S.

—— (1998) **Practice parameters for the assessment and treatment of children and adolescents with language and learning disorders**. *Journal of the American Academy of Child and Adolescent Psychiatry*, **37**(suppl.), 46S–62S.

—— (1998) **Practice parameters for the assessment and treatment of children and adolescents with depressive disorders**. *Journal of the American Academy of Child and Adolescent Psychiatry*, **37** (suppl.), 63S–83S.

Books

Wilkinson I (1998) ***Child and Family Assessment: Clinical Guidelines for Practitioners*** (2nd edn). London: Routledge.

Attachment disorders

Systematic reviews and meta-analyses

Fox N A, Kimmerly N L & Schafer W D (1991) **Attachment to mother/ attachment to father**. A meta-analysis. *Child Development*, **62**, 210–255.

Goldsmith H H & Alansky J A (1987) **Maternal and infant temperamental predictors of attachment: a meta-analytic review**. *Journal of Consulting and Clinical Psychology*, **55**, 805–816.

Van-Ijzendoorn M H, Juffer F & Duyvesteyn M G C (1996) **Breaking the intergenerational cycle of insecure attachment: a review of the effects of attachment-based interventions on maternal sensitivity and infant security**. *Annual Progress in Child Psychiatry and Child Development*, 157–183.

——, Marinus H & Bakermans-Kranenburg M J (1996) **Attachment representations in mothers, fathers, adolescents and clinical groups: a meta-analytic search for normative data**. *Journal of Consulting and Clinical Psychology*, **64**, 8–21.

——, ——, Goldberg S, *et al* (1992) **The relative effects of maternal and child problems on the quality of attachment: a meta-analysis of attachment in clinical samples**. *Child Development*, **63**, 840–858.

Books

Belsky J & Cassidy J (1994) **Attachment: theory and evidence**. In ***Development Through Life: a Handbook for Clinicians*** (eds M Rutter & D Hay), pp. 373–402. Oxford: Blackwell Scientific.

Electroconvulsive therapy

Systematic reviews and meta-analyses

Baldwin S & Oxlad M (1996) **Multiple case sampling of ECT administration to minors: review and meta-analysis**. *Journal of Mental Health*, **5**, 451–463.

Rey J M & Walter G (1997) **Half a century of ECT use in young people**. *American Journal of Psychiatry*, **154**, 595–602.

Reviews

Bertagnoli M & Borchardt C M (1990) **A review of ECT for children and adolescents**. *Journal of the American Academy of Child and Adolescent Psychiatry*, **29**, 302–307.

Other

Duffett R, Hill P & Lelliott P (1999) **Use of electroconvulsive therapy in young people**. *British Journal of Psychiatry*, **175**, 228–230.

Prevention and mental health promotion

Systematic reviews and meta-analyses

Durlak J A & Wells A M (1997) **Primary prevention mental health programs for children and adolescents: a meta-analytic review**. *American Journal of Community Psychology*, **25**, 115–152.

Hodnett E D & Roberts I (1999) **Home-based social support for socially disadvantaged mothers**. Cochrane Review. In *The Cochrane Library*. Issue 4. Oxford: Update Software.

Zoritch B. & Roberts I (1999) **Day care for pre-school children**. Cochrane Review. In *The Cochrane Library*. Issue 1. Oxford: Update Software.

Clinical guidelines

Arthur B, Elster M D & Kuznets N J (1997) **Guidelines for adolescent preventive services (GAPS)**. *Archives of Pediatric Adolescent Medicine*, **151**, 123–128.

Reports

Moore A & Gray A M (1995) **Evidence-based prevention**. *Bandolier*, October, 20–23.

Tuiford S, Delaney F & Vogels M (1997) *Effectiveness of Mental Health Promotion Interventions: a Review*. London: Health Education Authority.

Appendix i: Search strategies

Search strategy to identify randomised controlled trials in Medline

Silver Platter Format (version 3.10)

From: Dickersin K, Scherer R & Lefebvre C (1994) **Identifying relevant studies for systematic reviews.** *British Medical Journal,* **309**, 1286–1291.

#1 (Subject search strategy)

#2 (TG= ANIMAL) not ((TG=HUMAN) and (TG=ANIMAL))

#3 #1 not #2

#4 RANDOMISED–CONTROLLED–TRIAL in PT

#5 CONTROLLED–CLINICAL–TRIAL in PT

#6 RANDOMISED–CONTROLLED–TRIALS

#7 RANDOM–ALLOCATION

#8 DOUBLE–BLIND–METHOD

#9 SINGLE–BLIND–METHOD

#10 CLINICAL–TRIAL in PT

#11 explode CLINICAL–TRIALS/ ALL SUBHEADINGS

#12 (clin* near trial*) in TI

#13 (clin* near trial*) in AB

#14 (singl* or doubl* or trebl* or tripl*) near (blind* or mask*)

#15 (#14 in TI) or (#14 in AB)

#16 PLACEBOS

#17 placebo* in TI

#18 placebo* in AB

#19 random* in TI

#20 random* in AB

#21 RESEARCH–DESIGN

#22 TG=COMPARATIVE–STUDY

#23 explode EVALUATIONS–STUDIES/ ALL SUBHEADINGS

#24 FOLLOW–UP–STUDIES

#25 PROSPECTIVE–STUDIES

#26 control* or prospectiv* or volunteer*

#27 (#26 in TI) or (#26 in AB)

#28 #4 or #5 or #6 or #7 or #8 or #9

#29 #10 or #11 or #12 or #13 or #15 or #16 or #17 or #18 or #19 or #20 or #21

#30 #22 or #23 or #24 or #25 or #27

#31 #28 or #29 or #30

#32 #3 and #31

○ Upper case denotes controlled vocabulary.

○ Lower case denotes free-text terms.

○ Readers wishing to run this search strategy are recommended to seek the advice of a trained medical librarian.

From:

Dickersin K, Scherer R & Lefebvre C (1994) **Identifying relevant studies for systematic reviews.** *British Medical Journal,* **309**, 1286–1291.

#1   RANDOMISED CONTROLLED TRIAL.pt.
#2   CONTROLLED CLINICAL TRIAL.pt.
#3   RANDOMISED CONTROLLED TRIALS.sh.
#4   RANDOM ALLOCATION.sh.
#5   DOUBLE BLIND METHOD.sh.
#6   SINGLE–BLIND METHOD.sh.
#7   or/#1–6
#8   ANIMAL.sh. not HUMAN.sh.
#9   #7 not #8

#10   CLINICAL TRIAL.pt.
#11   exp CLINICAL TRIALS
#12   (clin$ adj25 trial$).ti,ab.
#13   ((singl$ or doubl$ or trebl$ or tripl$) adj25 (blind$ or mask$)).ti,ab.
#14   PLACEBOS.sh.
#15   placebo$.ti,ab.
#16   random$.ti,ab.
#17   RESEARCH DESIGN.sh.
#18   or/#10–17
#19   #18 not #8
#20   #19 not #9

#21   COMPARATIVE STUDY.sh.
#22   exp EVALUATION STUDIES
#23   FOLLOW UP STUDIES.sh.
#24   PROSPECTIVE STUDIES.sh.
#25   (control$ or prospectiv$ or volunteer$).ti,ab.
#26   or/#21–25
#27   #26 not #8
#28   #26 not (#9 or #20)
#29   #9 or #20 or #28

    O Upper case denotes controlled vocabulary.

    O Lower case denotes free-text terms.

    O Readers wishing to run this search strategy are recommended to seek the advice of a trained medical librarian.

Ovid version

Search strategy 1: high sensitivity, low precision

Best for the researcher keen to retrieve all systematic reviews while retaining a reasonable level of precision.

#1   meta.ab
#2   synthesis.ab
#3   literature.ab
#4   randomized.hw
#5   published.ab
#6   meta-analysis.pt
#7   extraction.ab
#8   trials.hw
#9   controlled.hw
#10 medline.ab
#11 selection.ab
#12 sources.ab
#13 trials.ab
#14 review.ab
#15   review.pt
#16 articles.ab
#17 reviewed.ab
#18 english.ab
#19 language.ab
#20 comment.pt
#21 letter.pt
#22 editorial.pt
#23 animal/
#24 human/
#25 #23 not (#23 and #24)
#26 (Your subject terms)
#27 #26 not (#20 or #21 or #22 or #25)
#28 or/#1–19
#29 #27 and #28

Search strategy 2: high precision, low sensitivity

Best for the busy searcher who has access only to Medline.

#1   medline.ab
#2   comment.pt
#3   letter.pt
#4   editorial.pt
#5   animal/
#6   human/
#7   #5 not (#5 and #6)
#8   (Your subject terms)
#9   #8 not (#2 or #3 or #4 or #7)
#10 #1 and #9

Appendix ii: critical appraisal tools

Critical appraisal tool: meta-analyses and systematic reviews (adapted from material produced by the Centre for Evidence-Based Mental Health)

Title of paper:
Author:
Source:
Date:

A. Are the results valid?

1. Is the question clearly focused?

○ What is being reviewed?

○ What is the population?

○ What is the exposure/intervention?

○ What is the outcome?

Comments

2. Is the search thorough? (Did the authors look for the appropriate sort of papers)

○ Bibliographic databases; years covered?

○ References in relevant articles?

○ Are the inclusion criteria appropriate?

Comments

3. Is the validity of included studies adequately assessed?

○ Reproducible, blind assessment?

○ Is missing information obtained from investigators?

○ Is publication bias an issue?

○ Has methodological quality been assessed?

○ Randomised controlled trials, cohort studies, case-control studies.

Comments

4. How big is the overall effect?

    ○ On what scale is the effect measured? (odds ratio, number needed to treat?)

Comments

5. Are the results consistent from study to study?

    ○ How sensitive are the results to changes in the way the review was done?

Comments

6. If the results of the review have been combined, was it reasonable to do so?

    ○ Were the results similar from study to study?

    ○ Are the results of the included studies clearly displayed?

    ○ Are the results of the different studies similar?

    ○ Are the reasons for any variations in results discussed?

Comments

7. How precise are the results?

    ○ Does the lower confidence limit include clinically relevant effects?

    ○ Does the upper confidence limit exclude clinically relevant effects?

Comments

C. Interpretation of the results – will they help in making decisions about patients?

8. Do conclusions flow from evidence that is reviewed?

Comments

9. Are subgroup analyses interpreted cautiously?

Comments

10. Can the conclusions and data be generalised to other settings? (Is the number needed to treat stated or should it be calculated?)

Comments

11. Were all important outcomes considered?

Comments

12. Are the benefits worth the harms and the costs?

Comments

Title of paper: . . . .
Author: . . . .
Source: . . . .
Date: . . . .

A. Are the results of this trial valid?

1. Are you using the right research paper to answer your particular question?

Comments

2. Was the group of patients clearly defined?

Consider:

O The population studied

O Comorbidity

O Classification used

O Outcomes measured

Comments

3. Was the assignment of patients to treatments randomised?

O Was the randomisation list concealed?

Comments

4. Were all patients who entered the trial accounted for at its conclusion?

Comments

5. Were they analysed in the groups to which they were randomised?

Comments

6. Were patients and clinicians kept 'blind' to which treatment was being received?

Comments

7. Aside from the experimental treatment, were the groups treated equally?

Comments

8. If a cross-over design was used were attempts made to reduce the carry-over effects?

○ Did the authors acknowledge that this was a potential problem?

○ Was an appropriate washout period used?

Comments

B. What are the results?

9. How large was the treatment effect?

○ See Guidance: calculating number needed to treat (page 96)

Comments

10. How precise is the estimate of treatment effect?

○ See Guidance: calculating confidence intervals (page 98)

Comments

C. What are the implications of this paper for local practice?

11. Are the results of this study generalisable to your patients?

○ Does your patient resemble those in the study?

○ What are your patient's preferences?

○ Are there alternative treatments available?

Comments

'Number needed to treat' (NNT) represents the number of patients you need to treat in order to prevent one negative outcome.

A worked example is included on the following page.

2.1 Establish the control event rate

The control event rate (CER) is the proportion of patients in the study's control group experiencing the observed negative event.

Enter the CER for your study in the box:

CER =

2.2 Establish the experimental event rate

The experimental event rate (EER) is the proportion of patients in the study's experimental group (i.e. the group receiving the experimental treatment) experiencing the observed negative event.

Enter the EER for your study in the box:

EER =

2.3 Calculate the absolute risk reduction

The absolute risk reduction (ARR) is the absolute difference in the risk of an adverse outcome between the control group and the experimental group. It is calculated by deducting the EER from the CER.

Perform this calculation now:

ARR =   (CER from above) –   (EER from above) =

2.4 Calculate the number needed to treat

The number needed to treat (NNT) is calculated by dividing the ARR into 1 and multiplying the result by 100. Perform this calculation now:

NNT = 1 /   (ARR from above) x 100 =

NNTs: worked example

Sample data

A population of 200 patients was divided into an experimental and a control group with 100 patients in each. The experimental group was given haloperidol in order to prevent recurrence of psychotic episodes. Ten patients in the experimental group experienced a psychotic episode during the period of the trial. Thirty-five patients in the control group experienced a psychotic episode during the period of the trial.

1. Establish the CER

35 patients experienced the event out of a population of 100, therefore the CER will be 35%.

CER = 35%

2. Establish the EER?

10 patients experienced the event out of a population of 100, therefore the EER will be 10%.

EER = 10%

3. Calculate the ARR

In this example, the CER equals 35% and the EER equals 10%.

ARR = 35 (CER from above) – 10 (EER from above) = 25%

4. Calculate the NNT

In our sample data, the ARR equals 25%.

NNT = 1/25 (ARR from above) x 100 = 4

The confidence interval (CI) gives the range within which we would expect the true value of a statistical measure to lie.

Most research studies use a CI of 95%, for example, an NNT of 10 with a 95% CI of 5 to 15 would give us 95% confidence that the true NNT value was between 5 and 15.

3.1 The Formula

The formula for calculating a 95% Confidence Interval on an NNT is:

$$+/-1.96 \sqrt{\frac{CER \times (1-CER)}{n \text{ of contol patients}} + \frac{EER \times (1-EER)}{n \text{ of experimental patients}}}$$

Please note: in the formula the CER and EER are expressed as fractions, rather than percentages. For example, a 25% CER is expressed as 0.25.

$$+/-1.96 \sqrt{\frac{... \times (1-...\ )}{...} + \frac{... \times (1-...\ \ \ \ )}{...}}$$

This will give you the percentage range within which the truly accurate NNT can be found. The smaller the percentage, the more confident you can be that the NNT is accurate.

Clinical guidelines (adapted from material from the Centre for Evidence-Based Menta Health

Title of paper: . . . .
Author: . . . .
Source: . . . .
Date: . . . .

A. Are the recommendations in this guideline valid?

Comments

1. Were all important decision options and outcomes clearly specified?

2. Was the evidence relevant to each decision option identified, validated and combined in a sensible and explicit way?

3. Are the relative preferences that key stakeholders attach to the outcomes of decisions (including benefits, risks and costs) identified and explicitly considered?

4. Is the guideline resistant to clinically sensible variations in practice?

B. Is this guideline potentially useful?

5. Does this guideline offer an opportunity for significant improvement in the quality of health care practice?

Comments

   ○ Is there a large variation in current practice?

   ○ Does the guideline contain new evidence (or old evidence not yet acted upon) that could have an important impact on management?

   ○ Would the guideline affect the management of so many people, or concern individuals at such high risk, or involve such high costs that even small changes in practice could have major impacts on health outcomes or resources?

6. **What barriers exist to its implementation?**

   O Can they be overcome?

7. **Can you collaborate with key colleagues to implement the guideline?**

8. **Can you meet the variety of conditions which will determine the success or failure of implementing the guideline? For example:**

   O Has the evidence been collated by a respected body (e.g. a rigourously developed clinical practice guideline from a Royal College)?

   O Are local opinion leaders already implementing the strategy?

   O Have you received consistent information from all relevant sources?

   O Has there been an opportunity for individual discussions about the strategy with a respected colleague/ authority?

   O Has a 'user-friendly' format for the guidelines been developed? (It may require local adoption)

   O Can you implement the guideline within a target group of clinicians (without the need for extensive outside collaboration)?

   O Does the guideline represent a conflict of interest with patient and community expectations, economic incentives, administrative incentives etc?

Comments

Additional comments

Criteria for the evaluation of qualitative research papers (adapted from the British Sociological Association Medical Sociology Group Guidelines, 1996)

1. Are the methods of the research appropriate to the nature of the question being asked?

○ Does the research seek to understand processes or structures, or illuminate subjective experiences or meanings?

○ Are the categories or groups being examined of a type which cannot be preselected, or the possible outcomes cannot be specified in advance?

○ Could a quantitative approach have addressed the issue better?

Comments

2. Is the connection to an existing body of knowledge or theory clear?

○ Is there adequate reference to the literature?

○ Does the work cohere with, or critically address, existing theory?

Comments

Methods

3. Are there clear accounts of the criteria used for the selection of subjects for study, and of the data collection and analysis?

4. Is the selection of cases or participants theoretically justified?

○ The unit of research may be people, or events, institutions, samples of natural behaviour, conversations, written material, etc. In any case, while random sampling may not be appropriate, is it nevertheless clear what population the sample refers to?

Comments

4. (cont.)

- ○ Is consideration given to whether the units chosen were unusual in some important way?

5. Does the sensitivity of the methods match the needs of the research questions?

- ○ Does the method accept the implications of an approach which respects the perceptions of those studied?

- ○ To what extent are any definitions or agendas taken for granted, rather than being critically examined or left open?

- ○ Are the limitations of any structured interview method considered?

6. Has the relationship between fieldworkers and subjects been considered, and is there evidence that the research was presented and explained to its subjects?

- ○ If more than one worker was involved, has comparability been considered?

- ○ Is there evidence about how the subjects perceived the research?

- ○ Is there evidence about how any group processes were conducted?

7. Was the data collection and record keeping systematic?

- ○ Were careful records kept?

- ○ Is the evidence available for independent examination?

- ○ Were full records or transcripts of conversations used if appropriate?

Comments

8. Is reference made to accepted procedures for analysis?

Comments

○ Is it clear how the analysis was done? (detailed repetition of how to perform standard procedures ought not to be expected)

○ Has its reliability been considered, ideally by independent repetition?

9. How systematic is the analysis?

○ What steps were taken to guard against selectivity in the use of data?

○ In research with individuals, is it clear that there has not been selection of some cases and ignoring of less interesting ones? In group research, are all categories of opinion taken into account?

10. Is there adequate discussion of how themes, concepts and categories were derived from the data?

○ It is sometimes inevitable that externally given or predetermined descriptive categories are used, but have they been examined for their real meaning or any possible ambiguities?

11. Is there adequate discussion of the evidence both for and against the researcher's arguments?

○ Is negative data given?

○ Has there been any search for cases which might refute the conclusions?

12. Have measures been taken to test the validity of the findings?

○ Have methods such as feeding them back to the respondents, triangulation, or procedures such as grounded theory been used?

13. Have any steps been taken to see whether the analysis would be comprehensible to the participants, if this is possible and relevant?

○ Has the meaning of their accounts been explored with respondents?

○ Have apparent anomalies and contradictions been discussed with them, rather than assumptions been made?

Comments

Presentation

14. Is the research clearly contextualised?

○ Has all the relevant information about the setting and subjects been supplied?

○ Are the variables being studied integrated in their social context, rather then abstracted and decontextualised?

15. Are the data presented systematically?

○ Are quotations, fieldnotes etc. identified in a way which enables the reader to judge the range of evidence used?

16. Is a clear distinction made between the data and its interpretation?

○ Do the conclusions follow from the data?

17. Is sufficient of the original evidence presented to satisfy the reader of the relationship between the evidence and the conclusions?

○ Though the presentation of discursive data is always going to require more space than numerical data, is the paper as concise as possible?

Comments

18. **Is the author's own position clearly stated?**

  ○ Is the researcher's perspective described?

  ○ Has the researcher examined his or her own role, possible bias and influence on the research?

19. **Are the results credible and appropriate?**

  ○ Do they address the research question(s)?

  ○ Are they plausible and coherent?

  ○ Are they important, either theoretically or practically, or trivial?

Comments

Ethics

20. **Have ethical issues been adequately considered?**

  ○ Has the issue of confidentiality been adequately dealt with?

  ○ Have the consequences of the research – including establishing relationships with the subjects, raising expectations, changing behaviour etc. – been considered?

Comments

Reference

British Sociological Association Medical Sociology Group (1996) *British Sociological Association Medical Sociology Group Guidelines. Criteria for Evaluation of Qualitative Research Papers*. London: Medical Sociology Group of the British Sociological Association.

Appendix iii: fax back to FOCUS

We hope the papers that we have included in this book will be of value to people who are keen to learn more about their subjects of interest. Please help us keep this record up-to-date by faxing any examples of secondary research that we may have missed. Thank you.

To: FOCUS Office

Fax: 020 7227 0850

Date:

From:

Subject

Title of article

Source (please provide a full reference)

Systematic review/ meta-analyses or clinical guideline or report?
(Please circle appropriate heading).

If you do not have access to a fax machine please send this form to:

The FOCUS Project
The Royal College of Psychiatrists' Research Unit
83 Victoria Street
London SW1H 0HW